My Daughter, Myself

An Unexpected Journey

My Daughter, Myself

AN UNEXPECTED JOURNEY

A Memoir

Linda Wolfe

GREENPOINT PRESS
NEW YORK, NY

Also by Linda Wolfe

The Murder of Dr. Chapman

Love Me To Death

Double Life

Wasted: The Preppie Murder

Private Practices: A Novel

The Cosmo Report: Women and Sex in the Eighties

*The Professor and the Prostitute: True Tales
of Murder and Madness*

Playing Around: Women and Extramarital Sex

The Cooking of the Caribbean Islands

The Literary Gourmet

For R.S.B. and M.J.B.

Copyright © 2013 by Linda Wolfe
All rights reserved.

LindaWolfe.com

No part of this book may be reproduced or transmitted in any form or by any
electronic or mechanical means, including photocopying, recording or by any
information storage and retrieval system, without the express written permission of
the publisher, except where permitted by law.

ISBN 978-0-9886968-1-5

Library of Congress Cataloging-in-Publication Data

Designed by Robert L. Lascaro, LascaroDesign.com
Book text set in Minion Pro, text drop caps, chapter titles and cover title
set in Schneidler

Greenpoint Press,
a division of New York Writers Resources
greenpointpress.org
PO Box 2062
Lenox Hill Station
New York, NY 10021

New York Writers Resources:
· newyorkwritersresources.com
· newyorkwritersworkshop.com
· greenpointpress.org
· ducts.org

Printed in the United States
on acid-free paper

Table of Contents

PART ONE

EVERY MOTHER'S NIGHTMARE

CHAPTER ONE

Mother's Day

THE NIGHTMARE BEGAN, although I didn't recognize it at the time, on a Mother's Day weekend a few years ago. I was in San Antonio, Texas, having flown down from my home in New York City to spend the weekend with my daughter, Jessica, her husband, and their children, my two young granddaughters. Sometime in the black-as-pitch hours before dawn on Sunday morning, Jessica was startled into wakefulness by a splitting headache. She went to the bathroom, used the toilet, splashed water on her face, and was headed back to bed, when suddenly one of her legs gave way beneath her and she fell.

Asleep in the guest bedroom across the hallway, I was not aware of this. Nor was I aware that Jessica pulled herself up from the floor and, convinced she'd feel better if she got some more rest, lay down in the queen-sized bed she and her husband shared, curled up beside Jon's slumbering body, and went back to sleep.

I didn't know that when she woke up again it was light out

and her head was still hurting, only now it was hurting so much it was making her nauseous. I didn't hear her gagging in her bathroom or dialing her doctor's office, didn't know that a covering doctor, upon learning her symptoms, told her to go at once to an emergency room. Nor did I hear her discuss with Jon which emergency room to go to—the one where her doctor practiced, or the one closer to home, where they'd taken their elder daughter when she'd gotten a cut that needed stitches.

We'd had a wonderful weekend until then. My plane had come in late on Friday night. Jon and the children were already in bed, but Jessica had waited up for me. Thirty-eight years old, she was slender and tall, with an olive-tinted complexion and brown eyes that sparkled beneath twin scimitars of dense eyebrows. She'd looked especially pretty that night, her thick chestnut hair newly bobbed to a fashionable shoulder length. She'd cut it, she told me, for her new job—she was doing political and judicial research for Texas's Bexar County, whose capital is San Antonio. It was her first job in what was for her still a new hometown. The family had moved to San Antonio from Berkeley, California only a few months earlier, when Jon, who'd just gotten his Ph.D. in political science, had landed a teaching position at the San Antonio branch of the University of Texas. Jon liked his new job, Jessica had told me, and hers was perfect. She loved the work.

I'd gone to sleep happy for my daughter, and on Saturday gave her and Jon a break from childcare by playing "House" and "School" for hours with my grandchildren, three-year-old Miriam and eight-year-old Rachel. Saturday night I'd taken the family out to dinner at a restaurant my son-in-law wanted to try—a new Chinese place, festive with red and gold Good Luck banners. The menu was filled with an alluring array of dishes, and we had ordered expansively.

That dinner seemed to be what was on Jon's mind Sunday morning when I came downstairs for breakfast at about 8 a.m. "Jessica's not feeling well," he said to me as soon as I appeared. "She's been throwing up. I think maybe she's got food poisoning. Can you watch the girls while I take Jess over to the hospital to get her checked out?"

"Of course," I told him, pleased to be put in charge of my granddaughters; living so far away, I didn't get that assignment very often. But "food poisoning?" I asked Jon doubtfully. "None of the rest of us is sick."

"Yeah, but she ate the crabmeat and none of the rest of us did."

Then Jessica came downstairs. She looked awful, waxen as an Easter lily and all bent over, her normally strong and vertical stride a shuffling parenthesis. She grabbed her wallet—her medical insurance card was inside it—and said goodbye to her daughters. A moment later she and Jon were gone, though not before she whispered to me, "Mom, I woke up with a headache in the middle of the night. But it wasn't just a normal headache. It was like the inside of my head was ripping apart."

∝∞

I discovered what time truly is that afternoon. A minute is 60 seconds. An hour is 3,600 seconds. A May afternoon is 21,600 seconds. All day, the seconds plodded funereally forward while I tried to keep the children distracted. They knew their mother wasn't feeling well, but Jon had told them it was nothing serious, and when he assured them it was just a stomachache and she'd be back in time for the Mother's Day celebration they'd been planning, they had accepted his explanation. I wasn't able to, not when she'd looked so dreadful. But for their sakes, I pretended not to worry and flung myself into round after round of let's-be-this or let's-be-that games, mostly chosen by Rachel, who was forever making up games and writing plays. Among her recent hits was "The Prince and the Bowling Ball," which featured a princess who puts a bowling ball under a visitor's pillow to determine whether he's really, as he says he is, a prince. I'd brought my video camera with me to Texas, and after lunch proposed that the girls act out the drama. "Grandpa Max will love it," I coaxed. "He feels bad that he couldn't come with me this weekend, and if we make him a movie, he'll be so happy."

It worked at first. But after an hour of gathering all the props—the crowns and cloaks and beads, the feather for the prince's hat, the large rubber ball that could serve as a bowling ball—Rachel suddenly turned sulky and refused to go on with the show. "We acted it out when we were in New York last time," she bawled. "Grandpa *saw it*. Grandma! Don't you *remember*?"

Was she feeling my anxiety? Was that what was making her so cranky? I couldn't be sure, but there was no diverting her. Miriam wailed but Rachel prevailed, and I decided we needed a change of venue. The afternoon had grown increasingly hot, and although going outdoors would be less comfortable than staying in the air-conditioned house—at least for me, who was unused to Texas torridity—I began to insist that we do something outside. Play ball? Make chalk drawings on the sidewalk?

The children grimaced, but I figured outdoor play would quiet them down, break up their quarrel. Besides, I wanted to be out front, where I could spot Jessica and Jon's Toyota the moment it rounded the corner.

"All right, Grandma," Rachel finally acquiesced, "but no playing ball and no drawing on the sidewalk." I took my cell phone outside with me. It was 2002; Jessica and Jon hadn't yet bought cell phones, but Jon had promised they'd call from the hospital after Jessica was seen by a doctor.

Once the girls and I were settled down in front of their house, Rachel devised a game that involved gathering twigs, pretending they were tantalizing toys and having Miriam, for whom the concept of money was a total mystery, "purchase" the imaginary toys with bits of rock and stone. It was an endless game, and an endless afternoon.

Around five o'clock, my two stepdaughters, Jude and Debby, called—Jude from California, Debby from Oregon. They were Max's children, ten and fifteen years older than Jessica. I'd come into them, as we always put it, when Jessica was an eight-year-old, but we'd been a family for so many years that they, too, felt like blood daughters. They were calling to wish both Jessica and me a happy Mother's Day. *Happy.* Talking to Jude and Debby, I made light of Jessica and Jon's absence. No point in worrying them. Maybe it *was* food poisoning. Maybe that headache *was* just a headache. Maybe I had exaggerated how pale Jessica had looked, how stooped. Sometimes, for a few moments at a time, I could talk myself into believing these things.

Around six o'clock the children began complaining that they were hungry, and I gave up waiting for the sight of the car and took them back into the house. I was searching through the refrigerator for something to fix for their supper and had my hand on a carton of eggs when the house phone rang. Eggs in tow, I raced to pick it up, slamming the fridge door shut with a foot. It *had* to be Jessica. Please let it be Jessica! My hands were shaking, and as I raised the receiver with one hand, the egg box slipped from the other, sending a flood of sticky yellow puddling onto the counter and trickling down to the floor.

"Mom?" I heard Jessica say. "I'm okay, Mom."

"Thank God!"

"I had every test known to woman, and the ER doctor says I'm all right. We're picking up something at the pizza place, and we'll be home right away."

I could tell she was in a hurry to get off the phone. I couldn't let her, not without knowing more. "What else did the doctor say, honey? I mean, why were you so sick this morning?"

"He said it was probably migraine."

"But you've never had migraine before."

"Yeah, but they did a spinal tap and a CT scan and they didn't find anything. So the doctor said that sometimes people develop migraine in their late thirties, and it was probably migraine. Listen, Mom, the pizza's ready. We'll be home in a few minutes, and I'll tell you all about it."

She hung up, and I went down on my knees, not praying, just wiping up eggs. She was okay. It was *migraine*. Nothing life-threatening about that.

⚮

Jessica looked a bit better when she got home—she'd been given painkillers and anti-nausea pills at the hospital—and she was in a hurry to eat. After she'd consumed her first slice of pizza and was reaching for her second, I commented that I was surprised she had an appetite after all she'd been through.

"I don't really have what you'd call an appetite," she said. "It's more like just a big hole in my stomach. From not having a bite in the past twenty-four hours."

"Of course."

"Besides, now that I know there's nothing serious wrong with me, I feel I *ought* to eat. To get my strength back."

The pills she'd received had taken away her nausea, and her head wasn't hurting. Still, after dinner she decided to go to bed early, though not before we had a little of the Mother's Day celebration the girls wanted. "We worked all *week* making stuff for you," they pleaded. What they'd made turned out to be glitter-or-namented flower vases they'd created at school and huge, sticker-bedecked cards they'd made at home.

I hugged the girls and Jessica kissed them, and then she produced a gift they'd helped her pick out for me—a necklace of jade beads—and I gave her the present I'd brought her from New York: a silky blue bathrobe. The gift-giving over, Jessica started upstairs, asking me to give the children the cake and ice cream they'd been promised and read them their bedtime stories.

"Is Mommy all better?" Rachel asked when I finished reading and shut off her lamp.

"I think so," I said. And I did. So did Jon. So did Jessica, though she left a message on her boss's phone that evening saying she'd been sick over the weekend and thought she'd best not come to work until Tuesday.

The following morning, Jon took the children to school while Jessica slept late. I got anxious waiting for her to appear. I was supposed to fly back to New York in the afternoon, and I wanted to see how she was so I could decide whether to keep the reservation or remain in Texas.

She didn't come down until eleven. I offered to make her French toast, but she declined, saying, "I'm a little nauseous again."

"Honey, I think I should cancel my flight."

"No, Mom. It's nothing serious. I just don't feel like eating. Stop fussing."

She was wearing the silky blue bathrobe, and she lay down on the couch. I sat beside her, automatically putting my palm on her forehead in that classic maternal gesture.

"No fever, Mom," Jessica protested. "I already checked."

"I'm glad I got you that robe," I sighed. "Seems to have come in handy."

"Maybe if you hadn't I wouldn't have gotten sick," Jessica teased, "because I wouldn't have had what to wear."

Jessica loved to tease me, and the fact that she was her usual playful self made me think she was right about there being nothing serious wrong with her. It's possible that I wanted to think this. I'd been working on a new book for the past two years, and the deadline for turning it in was fast approaching. I needed to get back to work on the manuscript if I was going to make it. Still, I was hesitant to leave. So I asked again, "Are you sure you don't want me to stay?"

"It'll be better for me if you don't. I'm still knocked out, and if you go, I can rest."

"You can rest even if I stay. I won't bother you."

"Yes, but you'll be here. And I'll feel I ought to entertain you."

"I don't need entertaining. I'll read a book."

"Mom, even this conversation is tiring me out. If you leave, I can go right back to bed and rest all day. Jon is taking the kids to the library after school."

Jessica had never been sick with anything more serious than a few stomach flus and bad colds. Her illness repertoire included nothing that hadn't been cured by staying home from school or work and waiting until whatever was messing up her system went away. It's the repertoire of the healthy. And she'd always been remarkably healthy.

"The girls love the library here," she said. "They'll be there all afternoon, and I'm sure I'll be better by the time they get home."

Better. Jessica's CT scan had been read while she was at the emergency room by a radiologist who'd reported to the doctor in charge that he'd seen nothing amiss. Neither Jessica nor Jon nor I knew then that this radiologist had been wrong. As was hospital practice, Jessica's CT scan had been reread a while later by a second radiologist who had detected a suspicious mass in her brain, which he described in his report as "a hyperdense appearance of the internal cerebral veins." None of us knew that, given his alarming finding, this second radiologist assumed that Jessica had already been admitted to the hospital, and thus, negligently, failed to pass his report along to the ER doctor, who had already sent Jessica home. We didn't find out any of this until much later, and, in my ignorance, I flew back to New York.

✑

I called Jessica as soon as I arrived home. "I'm okay," she said. "Just feeling a little bit tired."

"And the nausea?"

"It's back again," she sighed. "But just a little. Jon thinks I might have a stomach virus."

I called the next morning to see if she felt any better, but Jon said she was resting and couldn't talk to me. Nor, he added, could he, because Rachel was throwing up. "It looks," he groaned, "as if they've both got a stomach virus."

Six hours later, I was sitting at my desk, working on my book, *The Murder of Dr. Chapman,* when the phone rang. I picked it up to hear Jon, his voice cracking, say, "Jessica's sick. Very sick. She's got a massive blood clot in her brain."

Jon's words took him only an instant to speak, but in that instant the orbit in which my days had been spinning gave way, and all my plans and expectations crumbled to dust.

⨯⨯⨯

Jessica had had a stroke. I knew virtually nothing about stroke at the time, had always assumed it was a disease of the elderly. How could my healthy 38-year-old daughter have had a stroke? Later, I would plunge into finding out as much as I could about stroke, learning that it assaults some 800,000 Americans a year, killing about 17 percent of them and damaging the lives of many who survive: leaving some partially paralyzed, some mute, some robbed of all ability to respond to the world around them. Later, I would find out that while the primary victims of stroke are, indeed, people over 65, some 10 to 15 percent of stroke victims are, like Jessica, under the age of 45. And perhaps because many ER doctors receive only minimal training in neurology, if any at all, a recent study found that one out of every seven young stroke victims is given a misdiagnosis. These patients are told that they've drunk too much alcohol, or that they have vertigo or an inner ear infection, or—like Jessica—that they've developed migraine. After which they are sent home without receiving the kind of treatment that could prevent death, or a life forever marred by impairment.

Strokes, I would also discover, result from an interruption of blood flow to the brain. The majority of interruptions are caused by a clot developing within a blood vessel either in the brain itself or in some other part of the body, generally the heart or the large arteries of the neck and upper chest. The clot clogs the vessel and, depending on whether it is in an artery or a vein, prevents blood from reaching or leaving brain tissue. If blood fails to arrive, brain tissue is deprived of its principal sustenance: oxygen. If blood can't leave—flow freely out—there is a build-up of pressure that could crush the brain within the skull.

Jessica, I would find out, had suffered this last kind of stroke. But that all came later, long after I learned that she had come downstairs sometime between my morning call to her and Jon's six p.m. call to me and wandered unsteadily into the laundry room. When Jon asked her why she was going there, she couldn't say, and when he began quizzing her about simple things, she couldn't supply answers. She couldn't even tell him the age of their daughter Rachel, home from school because of her stomachache.

That's when Jon had bundled Jessica and Rachel, too young to stay home alone, into the Toyota and sped to the hospital. There, Jessica's disorientation had been so apparent that even Rachel remarked on it to the admitting nurse. "I think," she told the nurse, "Mommy's brain is asleep."

✑

Jessica was my only child. Bright and energetic, she'd gotten a job in Washington, D.C. as a staff assistant to a New York congressman after graduating from college. Two years later she began working for a small federal agency, writing and editing many of its publications. When she and Jon moved to San Francisco, she took a position with San Francisco's Chamber of Commerce. At first she did research and organized lobbying trips, but gradually she assumed a more visible and public role, testifying at hearings, lobbying the state legislature, and being introduced to the Mayor at a press conference announcing San Francisco's first-place ranking on a *Fortune* magazine list of "top cities for business" as the person whose responses to the magazine's questionnaire made the honor happen. Deeply interested in public affairs, she'd shaped a career for herself that supported those interests and had become a woman of confidence and consequence.

This not only delighted but awed me, for she'd been uncommonly shy as a child and teenager. Extreme shyness runs in our family. My father suffered from it until he reached his mid-forties; I myself, until my late thirties. Jessica fought against—and overcame—this debilitating genetic inheritance while still in high school.

She approached the task with persistence, devouring self-help books in an effort to master techniques for overcoming shyness and, despite being afraid of emoting in front of others, accepting a role in a class production of scenes from "The Importance of Being Earnest."

"Back then, everyone was trying to draw me out of my shell," Jessica once wrote about the experience. "But it was only when I appeared on stage, exclaiming in my most preposterous English accent, 'My own Ernest! ...that name has a music of its own. It produces *vibrations*,' that I began to discard the shell." Afterward, she said, "Nobody would have known me as the shy teenager I was. The drama teacher not only succeeded in drawing me out of my shell, he made me feel like a star."

She'd held onto that new confidence, taken it with her when she entered the world of work.

Jessica was also the center of my universe. Perhaps this was because all children are the center of the universe to their mothers. Or perhaps it was because when she was five years old, her father and I had separated, and Jessica and I had lived without him in that interdependent intimacy that often develops when a child and a single parent forge ahead together. We'd formed a bond that was impregnable, and it remained that way even though, after just a few years of single motherhood, I remarried.

The man I married, Max Pollack, was a professor of neuropsychology at a major university, a Renaissance man knowledgeable about art and music, literature and medicine, film and food, who had a penchant not just for weighty books but for silly things like wind-up toys. Max was home, watching television in another room, when Jon called that Tuesday evening and said Jessica had a clot in her brain. I must have cried out when Jon gave me this news, for almost at once Max picked up the extension and began firing off questions. "What hospital is she at? Has she been seen by her own doctor or just the emergency room staff? Where in her brain is the clot?"

With his scientific training, Max knew what to ask. I not only didn't know, but couldn't speak. My teeth were chattering so furiously I couldn't get words out.

Still, I understood the answers.

Jessica was back in the emergency room at North Central Baptist Hospital, the same hospital where on Sunday she'd been so casually told to go home.

Her internist, Dr. Randall Vanover, practiced at a different hospital and had not yet been apprised of her situation.

As to the clot, it was in a vein in the superior sagittal sinus, which runs like a highway divider along the middle of the head, from front to back. The phone shaking in my trembling hand, I listened silently to Max and Jon, still unable to get a word out. I heard Max say, "She needs to be seen by a top specialist. Not just by emergency people. Call Vanover, find out who he recommends, and ask him if she should be transferred to *his* hospital."

"Right," I heard Jon say.

"Right away," Max said. "And call us back as soon as you can."

Then Max was in the room with me, wrapping a sweater around my shoulders, and my teeth were no longer chattering, and I was digging into my file drawer.

"What are you doing?" Max asked.

"Looking for something," I whispered, my vocal chords working again—but barely. My hands were flinging files onto my desk, and Max was staring at me as if he was afraid that now that I'd found my voice I was losing my senses. "I know what I'm doing," I muttered. "I'm looking for the name of that guy who was a dean at the medical school in San Antonio."

Max glanced down at the clutter of files accumulating on the top of the desk and slowly began nodding his head. "Stanley Leff's friend," he said.

"Yes."

When Jessica and Jon moved to San Antonio, our friend Stanley had told us that his childhood buddy, Marvin Forland, lived there. "He's terrific," Stanley had said. "He'll help the kids find an internist. And a pediatrician for the girls. He'll even help them make friends. He knows everyone in San Antonio."

I'd passed the information along to Jessica, but she'd failed to act on Stanley's tip.

"Oh, Mom, stop nagging," she'd said to me only two months earlier when, for the fourth time since she'd moved, I'd asked if she'd looked up Stanley's friend yet. "Lots of friends gave us the names of people to look up in San Antonio, but we've been so busy getting settled, we haven't had time to follow through. Besides, I did call Stanley's friend after the last time you brought it up. No one answered, and I just haven't gotten around to trying him again."

I tried him. I found his number, dialed it, and when a man answered, got out, "Hello. I'm Linda Wolfe. Stan Leff's friend. You don't know me, but. But—oh, God—something awful has happened to my daughter."

I couldn't go on after that, so Max took the phone from me and began to talk to this stranger, this friend of a friend, someone who didn't know us from Adam, telling him in a rapid but calm manner what little we knew about what had happened and asking if we should fly down a consultant from New York.

Forland told Max that a New York doctor wasn't necessary, that San Antonio had a number of highly qualified neurologists and neurosurgeons. "Who's your daughter's internist?" he asked. "If he's a good man, he'll be able to put together a team of top specialists. Give me his name and I'll check him out and get right back to you."

The return call came moments later. "Randy Vanover's fine," Forland said. "He trained with us."

By "us" Forland meant the Medical School at the University of Texas Health Science Center in San Antonio. "If your daughter can be moved, she ought to be under Vanover's care at Northeast Baptist," he said.

There was no time to waste. Forland said he'd call our son-in-law and personally advise him about what to do.

By late that night, Jessica had been moved from North Central Baptist Hospital to Northeast Baptist Hospital, where she was admitted to intensive care and given the blood thinner heparin, and I had booked a flight to San Antonio. I'd also spoken with Jon several times, and with Dr. Holger Skerhut, the neurosurgeon Vanover had enlisted, who was now in charge of Jessica's case. "It's a dangerous situation," Skerhut said to me gravely. "Your daughter's got a lot of swelling in her brain—and if we go in and try to relieve it, she'll bleed to death."

⧜

Swelling in the brain. Stroke is a killer, the fourth leading cause of death in the U.S., a camp follower that marches close behind heart disease, cancer and chronic lower respiratory disease. And one of its most hideous methods of killing is to make the brain self-destruct.

That organ, goes the common wisdom, is a magnificently engineered structure. Although its deepest and most essential innards are soft and mushy like Jell-O, their fragility is cushioned by cerebrospinal fluid, then protected by a tough membrane and the unyielding structure of bone that is the skull. The design, goes the common wisdom, is spectacular because it makes the brain's protective casing virtually impenetrable. But the fact is that sometimes, as in Jessica's case, that very impenetrability forebodes disaster. The swelling caused by a clot or hemorrhage creates enormous internal pressure. That pressure, unrelieved, can set off a kind of inner explosion that shuts down the brain's neural pathways, including those that control vital functions. Breathing and heartbeat can be stopped. "It's the same as being hanged," a British doctor told writer and stroke victim Robert McCrum.

Jessica was receiving heparin, but I gathered from my conversation with Dr. Skerhut that the blood thinner was being administered in a desperate but less than promising attempt to ward off looming disaster.

"If surgery is out of the question," I said to Skerhut, "and the heparin doesn't work, what then?"

"We're watching her," was all he could tell me.

I arrived in San Antonio early the next afternoon. Jon and I had agreed that if he wasn't at the airport to meet me I should take a taxi directly to the hospital. But he was there, waiting for me at the end of the long corridor that led from the arrival gate to the baggage claim area. I didn't have to ask him how Jessica was. I took one look at him and I knew. He was crying, his shoulders heaving. I began crying, too. We embraced, and the two of us stood there sobbing, oblivious to the people hurrying past.

Jessica had worsened. All day she'd been steadily losing consciousness, her heart rate was somnolent, and she'd developed what her doctors called "left neglect." Although she had occasional periods of lucidity, she could no longer perceive anything on her left side, not even her own body. It was as if, to her, half of her had vanished.

Dr. Vanover had explained to Jon that this was the result of the initial clot's having grown ever larger. Like a logjam in a river, an untended clot in a vein keeps expanding by gathering deposits to itself, and Jessica's clot was now impinging on her frontal lobes. Vanover had also informed Jon that the neurological team felt there was no alternative but to give Jessica tPA—tissue plasminogen activator—a powerful anticoagulant that has to be dripped through a surgically implanted catheter directly into the brain, right into the site of a clot.

The drug is relatively safe if administered within the very first hours of the first symptoms of a stroke, when it can dissolve a clot without the risk of excessive bleeding. But few people receive it in those first hours. Partly this is because few people who experience the numbness, nausea and acute headache that are classic signs of stroke recognize what is happening to them. Like Jessica, thinking that they'll feel better after a few hours of rest or sleep, they go to bed instead of rushing as fast as they can to a hospital. But even those who suspect they may be having a stroke and manage to get themselves to a hospital quickly may not receive tPA early in the course of their strokes.

For one thing, before tPA can be administered, a patient must have a CT scan. Some hospitals don't have scanning machines. Some that do can't afford to employ technicians round-the-clock, so a patient may arrive when there's no one available to handle the machine. For another thing, the scan must be read, and a neuro-surgeon must be available to administer the drug promptly once its need has been established. Some hospitals employ radiologists who are unskilled at reading brain scans, as happened in Jessica's case. Still others don't have a neurosurgeon on call.

Giving tPA late in the course of a stroke is a different matter altogether. The drug, a genetically engineered substance, becomes a threat as dangerous as the condition it is used to treat, for it can cause severe hemorrhaging; and while scientists have been trying to come up with other clot-busting agents, and a couple have shown promise, none has as yet advanced beyond the research stage.

The doctors at Northeast Baptist had explained the dangers of tPA to Jon. They'd explained, too, that they believed that without it, Jessica was a goner.

⟋⟍

"I told them to go ahead," Jon told me as we stood weeping in the airport. "They said they'd take her to the operating room right away, and made me leave. That's all I can tell you. I came to get you as soon as they took her."

We were leaning on each other like two drunks.

Then, "Let's get going," Jon said, breaking away and grabbing my suitcase. "They could be bringing her back from the operating room any minute now."

We scurried to the parking lot, leaped into the Toyota and sped down a tangle of highways. My eyes caught a blur of gas stations and roadside eateries and, looming like temples above these earthbound structures, the occasional skyscraping, glass-sheathed bank building. I leaned forward in the car, as if by tilting my body I could make the vehicle go faster. I wanted desperately to see Jessica. To be with her when she came out of surgery. To hold her hand. To touch her poor head. To be there for her. Sure, she had Jon. But I was her mother. When people are sick, don't they always want their mothers? A friend once told me that his 97-year-old great aunt, who'd despised her withholding mother for years, had begun, on her deathbed, to cry out imploringly, "Mama! Mama!" The story had made me shiver.

"We're here," Jon broke into my thoughts, pulling into the hospital parking lot with a great squealing of the brakes. We opened our doors, and the San Antonio heat exploded in our faces. Slogging quickly through it, we whirled through rotating glass doors and sped down a maze of corridors. I had no idea where I was going. I just trailed Jon blindly until finally we came to a pavilion marked "Surgical Intensive Care Unit" and propelled ourselves through the unit's swinging doors into a large reception area.

I was panting and stood still to catch my breath. I saw a kindly looking nurse at a front desk, a few huddled groups of elderly, teary-eyed men and women, and an elevator at the back of the room that was disgorging a swarm of white-coated figures. The swarm began running toward an inner doorway, and suddenly Jon blanched. "They're going to Jessica's cubicle!" he cried out. "Something's happened!" He broke away from me, and he too began running—but at the entrance to Jessica's white-curtained cubicle he was pushed aside and denied entry.

So much of what we were told afterward is a swirl in my mind. Only bits and pieces stick out, like splinters from sore flesh. Jessica had been brought down from surgery just before we arrived. Almost immediately, she'd had a seizure. The tPA, it seemed, had begun doing its job, had started dissolving her perilous blood clot, but it had also quickly manifested its malevolent aspect: its ability to make a clot turn into a torrent of blood. Jessica had hemorrhaged. Blood had broken through its normal pathways in the brain, rupturing vessels and quickly shutting down her body's vital functions. Jessica was no longer breathing. Her heart was barely pumping. She was immobile. And in a coma.

∞

Someone came and told us all this. Was it Dr. Vanover? He was a soft-spoken, handsome Texan, tall and worried looking, who came out of Jessica's cubicle frequently to keep us informed of where things stood. Or maybe it was Dr. Skerhut, the neurosurgeon who had spoken so discouragingly to me on the phone the night before and whose very name sounded ominous. Or maybe it was the hospital chaplain, a round-faced man with a tight-lipped mouth who'd been summoned to the ICU to console and comfort Jon and me because, as we soon found out, the likely outcome of what had happened was that Jessica was going to die.

It was one of them. Or all three of them. We were rarely left alone in those first hours after my arrival. Nor were we permitted to see Jessica. Then, at last, a nurse appeared and said that now we could. "One at a time," she admonished.

Jon went first. He stayed in Jessica's cubicle a few minutes and emerged silent and drawn in upon himself. "You may not want to see her," he warned. But I did. I felt as pulled to her as if she were the moon and I a tide, unwitting and governed by forces beyond my control.

So I went into the cubicle. And there she was: my child, my baby, at first glance still lovely, asleep like the fairy tale princess, her slender arms stretched long at her sides, her thick dark hair cascading around her face. That face was turned to the far side of the room, and I had to go around the bed to see it fully. When I did, I saw that although her brown eyes were open wide, they were unseeing, vacant. She was hooked up to the usual array of machines and tubes. A ventilator was maintaining her breathing, a monitor was recording and displaying her sluggish heart rate and negligible blood pressure, intravenous lines were pumping antiseizure medications and steroids through her veins. But it was her eyes that brought me low. I was so shaken by the sight of them that blood seemed to ebb from my own brain, and I felt that the fearsome sight I had just beheld was going to haunt me and torment my soul the rest of my life.

The remainder of that day is a blur. I know that at some time Jon and I must have left the hospital and gone to relieve the neighbor who'd been staying with the children. I know we agreed not to say more to the girls than that their mother was still very sick, and that soon after we got home, I fed and bathed them and put them to bed, while Jon returned to the hospital. I know he came in very late with no news, and we tried to calm our nerves by sitting in the kitchen and having a Jack Daniels together. It was cool in the kitchen. Jessica had been delighted with the brass-trimmed overhead fans that softly and busily kept the air-conditioning circulating. Jessica had been so pleased by the whole room: big enough for a large refrigerator, a dishwasher, a table that could comfortably seat the whole family and even some guests—amenities they'd lacked in their California apartment.

Jon and I didn't say much, just listened to the fan and the clink of the ice in our glasses. I didn't know about him, but I was afraid to speak, afraid I might say something I'd later regret, might blame him for what had happened.

I like Jon, a basketball player, an ardent baseball fan, an admirer of Shakespeare and the Beatles. But I had for years held something against him. I felt it was his fault that my only child was living so far from me. I felt that while the two of them were working in D.C., he'd pushed Jessica into agreeing that it would be best for him to do his graduate studies at Berkeley, rather than at an East Coast university. No, Jessica had insisted to me, he hadn't pushed her. They'd made the decision together because Berkeley was the best school for his specialties—Congress and the Presidency. "As soon as he gets his degree, we'll come back East," she'd assured me.

But they hadn't come back East. When Jon finished his graduate studies and it was time to begin teaching, he'd chosen, from among several offers, UTSA, the San Antonio branch of the University of Texas. "It's a great position," Jessica told me. "The university's really good. The salary's decent. And at least we won't be out in the middle of nowhere, where the other schools that offered him jobs are. We'll be in a city, Mom. Even if it's not an East Coast city."

I understood that, too. Nevertheless, I'd never altogether forgiven Jon, Arizona-born and westward-minded. Nor had Max, for that matter. He'd already lost his two daughters to the West.

All of this raced through my mind as Jon and I sat there drinking, the two of us hoping to get woozy enough to be able to sleep.

Finally, Jon spoke. "One of us better get to the hospital first thing in the morning."

I nodded coolly.

"The girls have to be at their schools by 7:30. If you want, I'll take the early shift, drop them off at school, and go over to the hospital. You can sleep till you wake up and then meet me there."

"Take a taxi?"

"Yeah."

"I guess."

Jon was being thoughtful, but all I could think of was that if only he hadn't wanted to go to Berkeley, and then to San Antonio, if only he and Jessica had stayed in D.C., or better yet come to New York, she'd have been seen at a competent emergency room, a place where brilliant doctors competed to be on staff and where her devastating CT scan would have been properly read and acted upon, instead of at the godforsaken Texas emergency room from which she'd cavalierly been sent home to die.

⸜∞⸝

The following afternoon, Jessica's second day in the coma, Max arrived at the hospital. He'd taken a crack-of-dawn flight from New York. Jon's sister, Ruth, who lived in San Francisco, also arrived. So did Marvin Forland. I could tell by the deferential glances he received from the nurses at the reception desk that the dignified, gray-haired man who emerged from the cubicle area was Forland, had to be Forland. He didn't practice at this hospital, had never practiced here, even before his retirement, but he was famous in San Antonio medical circles—a legendary kidney specialist with an abiding interest in literature and ethics who had just helped establish the Center for Medical Humanities and Ethics at the University of Texas San Antonio Medical School.

"Are you Dr. Forland?" I asked, going up to the man.

"Marvin," he said, offering his hand. "I'm so sorry about your daughter."

"You've seen her?"

He nodded. "And Randy Vanover, too. It's not a pretty picture."

I knew from our mutual friend Stanley that Forland, who'd taught at the University of Chicago School of Medicine, had transplanted himself and his young family to Texas in the late 1960s, when San Antonio first opened a medical school. He'd started as Chief of Renal Services, and gone on to serve as the Department of Medicine's deputy chairman for clinical activities and director of its residency program, and ultimately as associate dean for clinical affairs. These were grand medical titles, but Stanley had assured me his old friend Marvin was one of the most modest and kindly individuals he'd ever known.

Stanley was right. Marvin remained with us for hours, though he didn't have to, though he wasn't yet our friend, was merely the friend of our friend.

They were hours of ever-increasing gloom, made darker by the reappearance of the tight-lipped chaplain. "It's time to call your minister," he said softly, and I felt my stomach do a somersault. "Or would you like me to?"

"We're Jewish," Jon said, his voice robotic.

"Your rabbi, then?" the chaplain asked.

Jon explained hastily that the synagogue he and Jessica had joined didn't currently have a rabbi, just a cantor who was acting as the rabbi until a new one could be hired.

"He'll do," the chaplain said. "Shall I call him for you?"

"No," Jon murmured. "I'll do it. I'll call."

An hour or so later, the cantor appeared. Broad-faced, with a luxuriant crest of hair, he looked like a short Bill Clinton, an impression reinforced after he clasped my hand between two of his and, looking into my eyes with a deeply earnest expression, said, "Ah, you must be Jessica's mother." Then, wasting no time, he quickly drew Jon aside and began asking him questions. Would Jessica prefer burial, he asked, or cremation?

Jon didn't know. He and Jessica were in their thirties. Burial versus cremation was not something to which their young minds had ever turned.

Perplexed and unnerved, Jon called me over. "Did Jessica ever say anything to you," he asked, "about wanting to be... If she were to die, someday to die... About wanting to be buried or cremated?"

I couldn't believe we were having this conversation, but, oddly enough, I thought I knew the answer.

Jessica's father, Joe Wolfe, had died when she was 17. He'd succumbed, very quickly, to pancreatic cancer. Joe and his second wife, Beverly, had been living in Washington, D.C., and during high school Jessica had frequently made the train trip down from New York to spend weekends with them. When Joe got sick, he was frank with her, and told her his doctors had given him just three to six months. But she had imagined a scenario in which her strong and revered father would confound the doctors and survive for many more years. One month after Joe's diagnosis, when we received a call from Bev saying he had died, Jessica went into shock, panting and shivering and crying bewilderedly, "It isn't three months yet." We got her breathing normally after a while, but nothing could stop the torrent of her tears all that day and the next, or the gloom that began to enfold my once-sunny daughter like a shroud. Yet the day after she returned from attending Joe's funeral and burial in D.C., the gloom dissolved sufficiently for her to feel able to attend school.

It was the ritual, she told me, that had made her feel better. There had been the gathering of Joe's D.C. relatives and friends, the admiring eulogies at the funeral, the rabbi's solemn incantation at the gravesite: "O God, full of compassion, you who dwell on high, grant perfect rest beneath your sheltering wings unto this soul who has gone into eternity." A teenager, Jessica had been comforted by those words; they were brand-new to her and had a pacifying effect they didn't always have on older people, who have heard them more times than they care to recall.

"Burial," I told Jon and the cantor. "I'm sure she would prefer burial."

That evening, Jon set his sister the task of calling family members and close friends to tell them what had happened and alert them to the possibility that a funeral might be imminent. Both he and I were too numb to make the calls ourselves. We understood the necessity, but the action was beyond us. Speaking to anyone but the little posse of family members already present was beyond us.

Ruth, herself the mother of two young children, made the phone calls from outside in the yard. She didn't want Jon's children to overhear her dire conversations. We'd eaten dinner with the children and had tried to avoid discussing Jessica. Indeed, we'd been preternaturally bent on not even mentioning her name. When we set the table, Ruth and I, unfamiliar with where things were kept, found ourselves starting to ask Rachel, "Where does Jessica keep the serving spoons? The pitcher? The napkins?" and quickly amending our questions to, "Where would we find the serving spoons? The pitcher? The napkins?" It was as if by avoiding using Jessica's name we could distract the children from thinking about her.

Only Jon had the courage to keep her name in play. He spoke about her several times as we sat at dinner, told Ruth it was Jessica who'd taught him his recipe for the spaghetti sauce we were eating, Jessica who'd taken the ravishing photo of the children that adorned the refrigerator. And later, at bedtime, when Rachel asked, "Is Mommy going to die?" he didn't lie, as I would have been tempted to do. He said, simply, "We don't know."

He had decided to be totally honest with the children. It was a decision I questioned at the time.

❧

Marvin Forland came to the hospital every day after that. One of us, Jon or I, was always there, sitting on the edge of a couch in a secluded corner of the ICU reception area, waiting for the rare and exceedingly brief turns we were given to go into Jessica's cubicle. I didn't look forward to my turns. I hated to see my inert child, the life I had brought into being now all but snuffed out, and often I was ready to leave the cubicle by the time a nurse came to shoo me away. Jon was different. He not only sat beside Jessica for as long as the nurses permitted, but sometimes even longer, sweet-talking her caregivers into letting him remain while they shifted Jessica onto this side or that, changed her intravenous fluids, made their notes in her chart. He read his book, a new doorstopper about Lyndon Johnson's years in the Senate. He read the *San Antonio Express-News*, sometimes reading an item aloud to his comatose wife. He told me it made him feel good to be with her, and that he often talked to her.

Could she hear him? Marvin said maybe she could.

❧

One day during that terrible week, a grim Dr. Skerhut told us that Jessica's chances of survival were exceedingly slim and that even if she did survive, it was likely she would be paralyzed and likely, too, that she would be severely neurologically impaired. The hemorrhage had caused too much damage to her frontal lobes to expect much else.

Irreversible brain damage occurs, he explained tersely, within 15 to 30 minutes of oxygen deprivation. Jessica's brain had been deprived of oxygen far longer than that.

Dr. Vanover was equally pessimistic. "Jessica may come out

of her coma," he said, "but if she does, she may not be the same person you knew before. Or even what you'd call a whole person."

Not the same person? Not the daughter I'd raised? The child who'd gone to bed each night with a ragged stuffed lion named Liony? The girl who'd perched for hours on her window seat, making intricate drawings of the buildings across the street? The young bride who'd worn on her wedding day the same beaded cap I'd worn when I married her father?

"What are you saying?" I asked Vanover, my voice a moan.

"Her personality could be changed. Or—or she mightn't have what you could call a personality."

"How could someone not have a personality?"

"It happens," Vanover murmured. He went on to explain that some coma victims emerge from their coma in a persistent vegetative state, able to breathe on their own but unable to think or reason—and that others emerge unable to breathe on their own or speak or move their limbs but apparently able to think and reason. "Locked in," he said. "Locked into their bodies."

I knew what he meant. I'd read Jean-Dominique Bauby's book, *The Diving Bell and the Butterfly*, which was eventually made into a movie. Bauby had written about being trapped in his body after a stroke. Or, rather, he'd communicated to a helper what he wanted to write, letter by letter, by blinking his left eye as his helper recited the French alphabet to indicate the correct letter. Bauby's mind had been alive, his thoughts vivid and complex, but except for that blinking eye, his body had been virtually turned to stone.

Such a thing couldn't happen to Jessica. Could it?

I asked, and Vanover nodded a dreadful yes.

❧

The doctors' words set us to pondering once again what Jessica might want—to be kept alive, no matter what, or to be allowed to die. Suppose we concluded she'd prefer not living if her fate was to exist in one of those fearsome states? Was terminating her life acceptable under Judaic law?

Marvin, who was a member of the synagogue to which Jon and Jessica belonged, suggested we look for answers in a book he lent us on the Jewish approach to medical ethics, *Matters of Life and Death* by Elliott N. Dorff. We read in it that as long ago as the time of Maimonides, the 12th century interpreter of Jewish law, people had wrestled with the question of whether it was acceptable to bring about the death of someone whose brain appeared to be dead. Maimonides believed that it was, postulating that if a man couldn't reason, he was no longer a creature made in God's image, and since he wasn't, he could be treated in the same fashion men treated animals, which also did not resemble God: like an animal, his life could be terminated. We also learned that many rabbis disagreed with Maimonides' opinion on this matter, because abiding by it could lead to serious abuses, like discontinuing treatment of the mentally ill. "They too," wrote the author, a rabbi and professor of philosophy, "do not exhibit the rational soul described by Maimonides." Therefore, the philosopher-rabbi advised, in order to guard against the possibility that an apparently brain-dead person is actually in a reversible coma, he or she should be kept alive by mechanical means "at least for some time."

But for how long? And what would Jessica want? As if picking at a scab, we spent the afternoon probing at unbearable questions.

❧

Jessica's medical records from that day noted, "Patient doesn't respond to verbal stimuli; patient opens eyes but not on command; patient withdraws to painful stimuli and reacts when turned. Pupils sluggish but reactive to light. Lungs are coarse."

Her condition was the same the next day. That was the day Jon suggested that Ruth, Max and I fly home and try to get a little rest.

"There's nothing you can do here," he said morosely. "And even if Jessica dies tomorrow, there's no way we could have the funeral for at least a couple of days."

Jon was thinking about the amount of time it would take for the people he would want at the funeral to assemble. We were that increasingly typical American family—scattered all over the country. His parents were in Arizona, his two brothers in New England. Ruth and her family lived in northern California. Jessica's only uncle and his wife lived in southern California. Her stepmother, Bev, and Bev's husband, Jim, lived in Maryland. Her stepsister Jude lived in California, her stepsister Debby and Debby's family in Oregon. Then there were Jessica's best friends. All of them were on the East Coast.

None of us wanted to leave, but Jon was right—we were tired. Bone-tired. Worn out with weeping and waiting. Moreover, it appeared that Jon, who declared he was sure he could manage for a few days with help just from neighbors and local friends, was feeling stressed by having us constantly underfoot. In view of this, we decided to take his advice and go home. We could get back in a matter of hours, should it be necessary.

After we made our decision, Max and I went back to the hospital to say goodbye to Jessica. I let him go into her cubicle first and sat in the waiting room with an unopened magazine on my lap. When Max reappeared, about five minutes later, he shook his head and gave me a thumbs down from across the room.

Nothing had changed. "One of the nurses came in," he said, coming over to me. "She told me she had to check Jessica's catheter and that I had to leave." Sitting down heavily, he took one of my hands between both of his and held it tightly.

We sat there holding hands and not speaking until we figured the nurse had probably finished with Jessica. My turn. I stood up. But then I stood still. It seemed cowardly, but I didn't want to go inside, didn't want what was probably going to be my last encounter with my child to be the sight of her with those vacant eyes and that inert body. Maybe if I didn't reinforce the vision by yet another visit to her bedside, it would dwindle in my consciousness. Maybe if I didn't reinforce it, I would remember her always the way she used to be, with her eyes sparkling and her body vigorous.

"I can't do it," I said to Max. "I can't go in there." I was crying. Ashamed.

He put his arms around me. "It's okay, honey," he said. "It's all right. We'll just go."

And we did, coming back to a dark and silent house, the kids and even Jon sound asleep.

❧

Ruth, Max and I left San Antonio the next day. Ruth flew to San Francisco, and Max and I departed, as we had arrived, on separate flights to New York. Max's took off in the morning, mine in the afternoon. I was zombie-like on the plane, unable to eat, to read, even to sleep, able only to stare out the window into endless meadows of clouds that obscured the earth below. Life as I'd known it had changed. I thought about Jessica's birth, how perfect a creature she'd seemed when I first held her in my arms, examining her wrinkly reddened face and spiky black hair. I thought about Jessica as a child, how bubbly and entertaining she'd been, how she'd come home from school and regale me with tales of her schoolmates—the boy who'd said the class should send toys not money to the poor children of Guatemala because if they sent money, "they'll just waste it on food," and the girl who'd told her, "Suzy is my best friend. But I hate her."

I couldn't bear remembering these things and told myself to stop and think about my grandchildren instead. When I finally succeeded in this effort, I ended up recalling that six months ago Rachel had written a play called "The Three Orphan Princesses," which she, a friend of hers, and little Miriam, then two-and-a-half, had performed for Jessica and me. I'd found it a puzzling play because there'd been no reference to the princesses having or not having parents. Why, I'd asked Rachel, was her play called "The

Three *Orphan* Princesses"?

"They were *supposed* to be orphans," Rachel had explained. "In the very first scene Miriam was supposed to say, 'Our life is really sad now that our Mommy has died.' But Miriam's scared of anything that has to do with dying. She's even scared of Snow White, and she wouldn't say the words. She just stood there pouting and wouldn't open her mouth."

Actors already on the stage—the living room rug—and audience already seated in the row of kitchen chairs set up to face it, the playwright had hurriedly changed the line, whispering to Miriam to say, "Our life is really sad now that it's raining out,' instead of the line that had scared her mute.

What would happen to Miriam if her mother died? How could she bear it? What would happen to Rachel? How could any of us bear it.

∞

When I traveled, I usually telephoned Max as soon as my plane landed, but this time I didn't feel like talking, not even to him. Encased in my grief, I slow-marched myself into the terminal. But what was the point of getting my luggage off the carousel? What was the point of heading back to our apartment? What was the point of having to tell friends what had happened, of trying to finish the book I'd been working on? What was the point of anything? Wherever I went, from now until such time as my days would be mercifully over, I would be bound by my grief, a frozen Antarctica of a woman.

I dragged my feet. The anonymity of the airport was somehow preferable to being at home, where I would have to confront Max's grief as well as my own and see reminders of Jessica in every room: the photos of her on the piano, the books she'd recommended to me on the living room shelves, the artwork she'd done as a child still adorning the walls of my study. I sat outside the terminal building across from the taxi line, cadging cigarettes from departing strangers—I'd given up smoking a year before, but all at once I craved nicotine. And then darkness fell and I dragged myself onto the taxi line, got into a cab and, somewhere between Newark and the Lincoln Tunnel, dialed Max.

I had barely murmured, "It's me," when he shouted into the phone, "Jon just called! Jessica spoke! She knows her name! She knows how many children she has!" ✍

CHAPTER TWO

The Great Mother, Son-in-Law Struggle

DESPAIR TO JOY. JOY TO DESPAIR. Despair back to joy. Joy back to despair. For me, the next few weeks weren't so much a roller coaster of emotions as a bullet train zooming back and forth between two fixed points. Jessica was out of her coma, but one day she slipped back into it. The day afterward, she again regained consciousness. The next day, she was completely unresponsive. The following day, she articulated in a faint whisper the name of the night nurse.

Jessica has no memory of these early stumbles toward soundness, these weeks when her life hung in the balance—when nurses had to turn her inert body every few hours to keep her from developing bedsores, and a hospital physiotherapist had to raise and lower each of her limbs and manipulate each of her fingers several times a day to keep her from developing circulatory problems. Calling himself, jokingly, a personal trainer, the physiotherapist advised Jon and me to emulate him and perform these same exercises on Jessica whenever we visited.

I had returned to San Antonio and was once again assisting Jon in the demanding business of juggling child care and domestic duties with hospital vigils. Did Jessica know who I was at the times Jon stayed at home with the children and I showed up at the hospital in his stead? Sometimes I found it impossible to tell. But at other times I was sure she did.

The first time was on a day when I entered her cubicle to find her awake and able to make eye contact with me when I sat in her line of vision, but still completely unable to move. I placed my fingers beneath her right thumb, intending to perform the exercises the physiotherapist had recommended, when suddenly I felt her move her thumb on her own. She ran it up and down and across *my* fingers, stroking the nails and the knuckles and slowly investigating the gold of my wedding circlet. She played with my fingers for a long time, gazing at me all the while. It was an exploration, and yet I experienced it as a kind of embrace—the most delicate embrace I had ever received.

Jessica's temperature was normal much of that day; her blood pressure, too. Jon brought a Get Well card drawn by Rachel, held it up where Jessica could see it, and she was able to read the message aloud in a weak but comprehensible whisper. The nurse told us that, earlier that day, she'd asked Jessica if she knew what year it was, and Jessica had said, faintly but correctly, "Two thousand and two."

I was so cheered by the news. It suggested that not only her eyesight but also her memory were intact. But the unfailingly gloomy Dr. Skerhut cautioned me against being too optimistic. "She's not out of the woods yet," he said. "Some patients start to recover after a stroke but then develop another blood clot. Or another hemorrhage. Or brain spasms. Or seizures. Some of these things can happen even weeks after a stroke."

I was living, in those days, every mother's nightmare: the fear that your child could die. To have a child is to be afraid of all manner of things: "of swimming pools," Joan Didion wrote in her memoir *Blue Nights*, "high-tension wires, lye under the sink, aspirin in the medicine cabinet ... rattlesnakes, riptides, landslides, strangers who appeared at the door, unexplained fevers, elevators without operators and empty hotel corridors." Fears like these come with the very territory of motherhood. But what lies behind them is a nightmare, the terror that you might lose your child while your own life went on. Persisted.

Not so very long ago this possibility was not just a nightmare or a frightening daydream, but an all too frequent reality. Poor Mary Lincoln lost three of her four sons. When her second son, Willie, died of typhoid and it looked like her third son, Tad, might die, too, Mary fell apart and was comforted by women friends who had also lost children, one of whom had lost *five*. Mothers in the centuries that preceded Mary Lincoln's era *expected* to lose several, if not all, of their children during their own lifetimes. Childbirth was perilous not just for mothers but for newborns. Fatal childhood diseases were prevalent, and while it can never have been easy to lose a child, women diarists of the 17th and 18th centuries often wrote about a child's death in a tone if not of acceptance, at least of resignation. But by Mary's time, losing children had become less commonplace, and to those of us who live in modern times, that horrific prospect has become the stuff of anxiety-fueled, terrifying imaginings. Now, for me, the nightmarish scenario had turned into a daily, an hourly possibility.

In an essay on sadness, Michel de Montaigne, who lost several children, wrote about "that bleak, dumb, and deaf stupor that benumbs us when accidents surpassing our endurance overwhelm us." Montaigne's words described me to a tee. I was numb. I was like a zombie, half-dead myself. Jon was a zombie, too. We tried our damnedest at least to appear to be the people we used to be. But we weren't those people. Not anymore.

We tried, too, not to step on one another's toes, or get on one another's nerves. But living under the same roof with a son-in-law—or with a mother-in-law—can be a trial even in the best of circumstances. We were living under the same roof in a circumstance that was making both of us exceedingly edgy and irritable. We were not the polite, considerate selves we had always presented to each other. We were becoming quick to fly off the handle.

I objected out loud to Jon's leaving garbage to molder in the kitchen pail instead of transferring it to one of the big trash cans in the garage. He objected out loud to my feeding the children snacks before dinner. I complained about his habit of turning on a baseball game as soon as he entered the house. He complained about my habit of turning up the air conditioning as soon as I entered.

❧

Two days after Jessica whispered the year correctly and 12 days after her stroke, Jon and I were sitting in the kitchen having lunch together when the phone rang. "Vanover," Jon whispered to me as he held the receiver to his ear. He was silent for a time, just listening, and then I heard him say, "How serious is it?"

I put my hand over my mouth, afraid I might cry out. The voice at the other end continued inaudibly until Jon said hurriedly, "Okay. Yes, of course," and hung up the phone.

"What was that about?" I asked, petrified.

"Jessica's got another clot. It's in her leg."

I freaked out. "Another clot!"

"Vanover says it's going to be okay. It could have been caused by her original condition. Or just by her having been in bed so long. Whatever, they're going to do a surgical procedure right away. Put a filter in the vein, a kind of plastic umbrella, to keep the clot from traveling up to her lungs." Sitting down again, Jon bit into the tortilla with melted cheese he'd been eating before the phone rang.

"A surgical procedure?" I said. "We've got to get to the hospital right away!"

"Why?" Jon asked, taking another bite of his tortilla.

"Because it's surgery!" Deep within me was a piece of ancestral information gleaned eons ago from my parents, or maybe it was my grandparents, that held that if a person underwent surgery, a family member had better be pacing the hospital corridor ready to hear from the surgeon's own lips whether the patient had survived.

"Vanover said it was a minor procedure," Jon said, and calmly took a long swallow from his mug of tea.

"I don't care!" I was hysterical, barely rational. How could anything be minor for someone in Jessica's condition?

Jon went on eating. I suppose he'd had his fill of panicky moments in the past two weeks, and, to him, this one didn't rise to the level of those he'd previously endured.

"All right, do what you want. I'll go myself," I announced, and flounced off to call a taxi. In my constant state of exhaustion and apprehensivness, I didn't trust myself to drive on a Texas superhighway, so I used taxis wherever I went. I'd become friendly with one cab driver in particular, a man who called himself Dean—his real name was Farudhin—and I knew that if I called, he'd come to get me as soon as he dropped off the passenger currently in his car.

I picked up the phone and began tapping in Dean's number.

"Forget it," Jon sighed. "I'll go. You stay with the kids."

It was the start of the Great Mother-In-Law/Son-In-Law Struggle, a battle that was to consume us in the next few weeks. But, that day, we didn't know what lay ahead. I knew just that Jon was doing what I'd wanted him to do. He knew only that I was pushing him to do something he didn't want to do.

Still, he did it: went to the hospital, spoke with Skerhut right after Jessica was brought down from surgery, and called me to say she was recovering nicely. A few hours later he came home and took charge of the children, freeing me to go to the hospital.

When I got there, Jessica was awake and alert, and, to my astonishment, she seemed even more physically improved than she'd been the day before. As I sat beside her, she moved not just her right thumb but all the fingers of her right hand. There was more, too. Shortly into my visit, she began moving her whole arm.

Up to her chest it went, down to her stomach, up to her chest, down to her stomach.

Would she keep improving? Relieved from my anxiety over the surgical procedure and filled with excitement over her new achievements, I called Max.

"Jessica's paralysis is diminishing!" I reported. "She can make her arm go up and down."

"No kidding?" Max said. "Oh my God, that's great, baby. You and Jon should get some champagne. Celebrate."

"I *am* going to celebrate. I'm going to buy some pies." The idea had come into my head at just that moment. I'd go to that bakery Marvin had told me about, Janie's Pie Factory, and get pies for the family. Marvin had said Janie was a rare creature for San Antonio: a purist of a baker who, with the help of two fellow cooks, peeled all the apples for the store's apple pies by hand.

Dean drove me over to the pie factory, which proved to be a tiny storefront establishment. When the apron-swathed, eponymous owner came to the counter to wait on me, I found myself suddenly babbling. I told Janie about my daughter, told her I was from New York, told her I'd served two stints as a restaurant reviewer for *New York* magazine, that I had two granddaughters I'd once taken to San Antonio's Korean neighborhood to try, despite faces wrinkled with suspicion, kimchi. I said whatever came into my head. I couldn't stop talking. I felt like a kind of Robinson Crusoe, long deprived of social interchange and newly discovering the joy of speaking to a fellow human being.

In an absolute frenzy of happiness, I purchased not just one but two apple pies and two cherry pies as well.

The children, Jon and I devoured most of them that night. We were partying.

❧

The next day gloom returned. Jessica was torpid. She had been running a low fever all week, but it had now shot up to 102 degrees, her heart rate was exceedingly high and her blood pressure exceedingly low. She lay still in the hospital bed, her arm no longer moving and her eyes rolled up into their sockets.

When he came by to check on his now visibly sicker patient, Skerhut didn't seem overly worried about the fever. "After a stroke," he said, "it takes a while for the body mechanism that regulates temperature to sort itself out." As for the unruly heart rate and blood pressure, he said they were the result of the treatment she was getting. "We had to dry your daughter out," he announced.

"Dry her out?" I stared at him, puzzled.

"We reduced the volume of her blood to prevent bleeding. So now her heart is crying out for more oxygen."

Skerhut was making my child's heart cry? I must have flashed him an accusatory look, for he quickly went on to assure me, "We've begun increasing the blood volume. But slowly. It has to be done very slowly. Because it's a tricky business. If you increase the volume too swiftly, it can cause a secondary stroke."

A secondary stroke! He'd warned me just the other day about poststroke complications. But I'd put his words out of my mind when Jessica began moving her arm. Now, the words were hammers pounding on the little anvil that was *my* heart. Yet, after checking Jessica's intubations and heart monitor, Skerhut expressed contentment with how the procedure was going. "We're on course," he informed me. And then, a man of few words and even less bedside manner, he hurried off to see another patient.

Still, despite his brusque manner, I didn't dislike the head of the team Vanover had put together. In fact, I rather liked the neurosurgeon. Or at least I felt grateful to him. He'd kept Jessica alive by *not* operating on her, and he was apparently doing his best to make sure she stayed alive. *He won't let Jessica die.* Despite all I'd been learning about stroke in the past couple of weeks, strokes and death were still inextricably linked in my mind, their connection having been forged long ago on that day in my childhood when news that Franklin Delano Roosevelt had died of a stroke came over the radio. My mother and many of the other housewives in our Brooklyn neighborhood had rushed out of their homes and, weeping, embraced one another on the street, as if by holding one another's flesh within their arms they could vanquish their grief.

At night, in Texas, I hugged the children that way, clung a little too long to their tiny frames when I kissed them goodnight. They clung to me, too, in that way. Especially Miriam. The games she made up increasingly featured a baby animal that didn't know how to fend for itself. "I'm a baby kitten," she'd say. "You be the Mama cat." Then she'd curl up on my lap, and tell me, "I just got born, so I don't know how to walk yet. You have to keep me here and pet me till I learn how to walk." Or, "I'm a baby bird. You be the Mama bird." And once again she'd climb up onto my lap. "Your lap is our nest," she'd instruct me. "I need to perch there and you need to pretend-feed me."

After much petting and pretend-feeding, I decided to advance the game, to teach the kitten how to pad about on all fours and the fledgling how to fly. Over and over, Miriam and I crawled from the kitchen to the living room and back, or we flapped our arms and "flew" through the house. Miriam giggled hilariously and got rowdy and forgot for minutes at a time that her mother hadn't been home for two weeks. Me too. But at night, after I turned off their bedroom lamps, I would find myself embracing both her and her sister with that overlong hug.

⚮

"Our health is a long and a regular work; but in a minute a canon batters all; overthrows all; demolishes all: a sickness unprevented ... destroys us in an instant." John Donne was writing in this passage from *Meditations Upon Our Human Condition* about the destruction of the person who experiences the unprevented sickness. But it seemed to me that I, too, had been destroyed, that the person now inhabiting my body was not the even-tempered me I had known myself to be. Instead, I was consumed with self-hatred and anger. I hated myself for having failed to realize on the day after Jessica's fateful visit to the emergency room that she was still sick; I was angry at myself for assuming she'd get better and flying back to New York.

I was angry at a lot of other people, too. I was angry at the radiologist at North Central Baptist who hadn't noticed the suspicious mass in Jessica's brain when he read her CT scan. I was angry at the radiologist who *had* noticed it but hadn't passed the finding along to the emergency room doctor. I was angry at the ER doctor because he'd sent Jessica home instead of admitting her to the hospital. I was angry at the friends who called and inquired about Jessica's habits before the stroke—Did she smoke? Do drugs? Overeat?—thinking they were asking innocuous questions. Their questions weren't, however, innocuous. When I said, no, Jessica had never done any of those things, my inquisitors' voices always held a trace of disappointment, as if they'd hoped to find a way to attribute my daughter's catastrophe to something she'd brought on herself. Something against which they might be able to immunize their own children.

Most of all, I was angry at Jon. He'd been there that day I'd gone back to New York. He'd come home from the library and seen that Jessica was still in bed. He'd seen that in the evening she didn't want to eat or even talk on the phone. He'd seen that at night, while he sat up late at the computer, she didn't once venture out of their bedroom. Why hadn't Jon figured out how sick she was? Why hadn't he gotten her to a hospital again before she became incoherent?

I was so angry that I would start provocative conversations with him. "Why can't I give the children their baths first?" I'd demand when he'd said they needed to go to bed immediately. "Why don't you shut off the game and turn on some music for a while?" when he'd said it was the eighth inning.

Once, when I was feeling especially sorry for myself, I said, "It'll be all right for you. You'll remarry." We were in the car on the way to the supermarket. He was driving, and he took his eyes off the road for a millisecond to cast me an astonished, pained look. I didn't need to see it to know that what I'd said was a despicable thing to say to a man grieving over the impending loss of a beloved wife, but I hadn't been able to help myself, and the words continued to slam out of me. "You'll find another wife. Men always do," I went on. "But, me, I'll never have another daughter."

Jon pulled into the enormous parking lot and just sat there behind the wheel, waiting for me to get over my tantrum. But I couldn't get over it, didn't want to get over it.

There are stages of grief. Everyone knows that. Everyone knows, too, that one of the stages is sheer blinding fury. It is almost impossible to control that fury, to recognize that when a dreaded thing happens, it may not be anyone's fault—that one's anger is more properly directed not at a person but at fate, at the hand of God or the hand the cards have dealt.

It is also almost impossible to control the surge of self-pity. "You'll remarry, and I'll lose my granddaughters, too," I flung at Jon.

"You'll never lose your granddaughters." His posture was rigid. His voice tightly controlled. "I promise you that whatever happens, you'll never lose them."

"Oh, sure," I snorted.

Jon had had enough. Ignoring me the way you ignore a two-year-old in a tantrum—he'd had plenty of practice at that—he opened the car door and headed alone into the supermarket.

❧

If I was waging a battle with Jon, Jessica was waging a battle with her body. She still had fever, a racing heart, and blood pressure that was frighteningly high, but despite all this, she remained conscious and fairly alert and finally began speaking again. Just two words: "yes" and "no." She delivered them in response to questions, and we had to lean in close to her inert body and put an ear to her mouth to hear. Still, we persisted with our questions, and also began embarking on monologues. Marvin, who continued to stop by Jessica's cubicle every day, had told us he was sure that, even when Jessica gazed into the distance and said nothing, she was hearing and understanding us. So we directed a steady stream of words at her, prattling on about our activities, the children' activities, the friends and family members who were calling to see how she was doing.

Our attempts at conversation remained strictly one-sided until many days after her stroke. But one afternoon, as I was discoursing upon having finally gotten up the courage to drive her car, she murmured a whole sentence. "It's a good car," she said.

Astounded by getting a response, I went on chattering. I said I'd driven the car to the supermarket and bought groceries, and that I was doing all kinds of things that were unusual for me to do at her house—not just driving and marketing, but washing clothes, sorting bed linens, sweeping floors.

"And taking out the garbage?" Jessica said, quite audibly.

Not only was she asking a question of her own but she was teasing me. Jon must have told her about our garbage fight.

"No," I told her. "I've been getting Jon to do it. I've been getting tough with him."

Jessica, who couldn't yet alter the fixed position of her head, let alone the expression on her face or the focus of her gaze, said, "Good idea."

I burst out laughing. It was the kind of wry comment Jessica always used to make. Dr. Vanover had warned us that, if and when Jessica came out of her coma, she might be a stranger. "Not the same person you knew before." But, that afternoon, I felt for the first time that, although trapped in the prison of her body with just that single partially mobile arm, Jessica was herself. Her humor was intact.

One day toward the end of May, I was entering the surgical intensive care unit when I saw both Dr. Vanover and Dr. Michael Oliver, the neurologist on Jessica's team, standing at the nurses' station. They seemed to be in the midst of an intense discussion. Yet when they noticed me, they broke away from their conversation and beckoned me over. "There's good news," Oliver said. "Jessica's latest MRI shows that the clot in her sagittal sinus is diminishing. The venous blood has found a channel through the clot."

"The blood is flowing out," Vanover added.

Oliver went on to explain that, in his opinion, it was now time to start Jessica on a daily regimen of Coumadin, the blood-thinning medication commonly given to people whose strokes have been caused by a blood clot. "If she doesn't get it," Oliver warned, "she'll be at risk for developing more clots."

Vanover's face clouded over. "But with it," he said, "she could develop another bleed in the brain."

"Well, of course, there's a risk either way," Oliver commented.

Vanover turned toward me. "What," he asked, "do *you* think would be the best course?"

"Yes. What's your view?" Oliver chimed in.

I didn't want to respond. I figured they didn't really want my opinion, were just chatting me up, practicing the new medicine—the one that has replaced the old "doctor knows best" ethos with which I grew up. Informed consent is today's model, and most doctors want patients and their families to know all about medical decisions and their possible complications and alternatives. In part, the new norm is a result of the antiauthoritarian forces that marked the late 20th century—the women's movement, the civil rights movement, the consumer advocacy movement. In part, it's the result of medicine's giant advances—the plethora of new medications, surgeries, equipment that have given doctors far more choices to make. And, in part, it's the result of doctors' fears of malpractice suits—they theorize that if they choose Course A over Course B and Course A backfires, patients and their families will be less likely to sue if they've been let in on the complexities and risks of the decision-making process.

Declining to offer an opinion, I just thanked Vanover and Oliver for explaining the drug's dangers to me. And, as it turned out, the choice wasn't up to them, either. Later that day, Skerhut, who was in charge of the case, decided the matter. No Coumadin yet.

❦

The San Antonio heat was building as May began to creep toward June. That heat was extraordinary. To step outside the icy, air-conditioned confines of the hospital was to feel your limbs encircled by a heat so strong it was like being bound, unable to move. I'd go outside sometimes, when a doctor or a nurse would ask me to leave Jessica's cubicle for a while, and I'd sit on a bench set beneath a spindly young Texas oak tree and smoke a cigarette. I'd taken up the bad but somehow comforting habit again after those hours of cadging smokes in the airport, and I had my own cigarettes now. Even under the oak it was so hot that I wondered how I was going to be able to negotiate the short but treeless distance back to the hospital's revolving door. Or how my daughter, truly unable to move, was going to negotiate the long distance back to health. Or if she was going to be able to.

Whenever I sat there, whenever I stopped moving about and just sat still, I was flooded with memories of Jessica. I thought about her as a young mother, hefting 15-month-old Rachel onto her shoulders and striding along Berkeley's Piedmont Avenue, and about her as a college student, studying French literature and being blown away by Balzac. I thought about her as a teenager, cooking a surprise Indian feast for me and Max—mulligatawny soup, chicken curry, yellow rice, eggplant chutney, raita, the works—and about her as a pre-teen, learning to ride a bike one Fire Island summer and falling with a great thud onto the cement walkway. I thought about the way she'd remounted, fallen again, remounted again, fallen once more, until eventually she'd pedaled ecstatically out of sight.

Would she ever carry a child again? Read French again? Cook again? Would she ever again ride a bike? *Walk*?

I wanted her back. I wanted her whole. I wanted her just the way she'd been before. I wasn't nearly as undemanding about what I wanted as Jon, who one night said to me in a voice like a sob, "I just want her back home. I don't care if she's in a wheelchair. People in wheelchairs can have terrific lives."

Now that the blood clot in Jessica's brain was diminishing, both Jon and I had some highly encouraging visits with her. Marvin had suggested we stimulate her with things we knew she loved, like music and poetry. Jon brought her a tape player, headphones, and a cassette he'd made of some of her favorite songs. When he placed the headphones over her ears and turned on the tape, she listened with profound concentration.

I brought her books of poems and one day read A.E. Housman aloud to her: *And while the sun and moon endure Luck's a chance, but trouble's sure....*

"That's one of my college textbooks," Jessica murmured, surprising me by recognizing the book's tattered cover.

Soon after, she dozed off. I'd gotten used to the way she slipped without fanfare in and out of alertness. Marvin had told me that a brain recovering from stroke requires inordinate amounts of rest.

Sometimes when she slept I tiptoed away. But on this day I was still sitting beside her bed when she awakened and suddenly began talking nonstop in her faint, whispery voice. I couldn't hear most of what she said, but at one point I distinctly heard her say, "I fell onto the floor," and realized she was trying to tell me what she remembered about what had happened to her.

"I know, I know," I tried to soothe her.

A moment later she spoke in a most urgent fashion, words tumbling out of her as if there was absolutely no way she could control them. "I need," she said, but what followed was inaudible to me. "I need," and once again she emitted a torrent of sentences. "I need," she said a third time, but whatever it was that she needed was inaudible.

"What? What do you need?" I was leaning over her, my ear practically pressed up against her mouth. What was she trying to tell me? Did she need the nurse? Was she in pain and wanting a painkiller? It was heartbreaking not to know what she was trying to say.

At last Jessica said a sentence I did understand, speaking the words slowly and a little more loudly. "I need to get out of here," she articulated. "What can I do to get out of here?" Her voice was little more than a whisper, but the imploring words were clear.

What could she do? I felt utterly impotent. I tried, "Rest. Rest, and work with the physiotherapist when he does the exercises with you."

She said in her breathy whisper, "And pray."

❧

I was keeping a journal, and my notes boomeranged between the upbeat and the dismal. When I got back from the hospital on the day Jessica talked at such length, I wrote, "May 30. Good day. Oh, such a good day! Jess talking a blue streak."

But the next day, May 31, I wrote, "Bad day. Jess not talking at all."

Not only was she less responsive that day, but her eyes kept rolling up in their sockets the way they'd done when she'd first emerged from her coma and when she'd had that high fever. Worse, several times her eyes came back to their normal position and she'd look right at me and stare. But she didn't seem to want, or be able, to say anything.

That night, Jon and I had a big blow-up—an inevitability, I suppose, given the harsh disappointment of the day. It began with Jon saying he wanted his mother to come down from Phoenix and help out with the children. But wasn't I doing that? Feeling about to be demoted, I huffed, "Having two grandmothers in one house is one grandmother too many." As if it were up to me, as if it were *my* house. I had lost all perspective.

"My mother will cook and clean and do the laundry."

"I'm doing that," I said defensively.

"Yes," my new adversary allowed. "But you don't *like* doing those things. My mother does." Indeed, his mother, Alice, a Bryn Mawr graduate, had long ago decided not to pursue a career and instead had chosen to devote most of her time and considerable energy to homemaking and rearing her four children. I have my share of professional competitiveness. You can't be a journalist without a goodly supply of the stuff, without the inner drive that makes you want to get the story before the Other Guy does and tell it with more style and edge than that Other Guy can. But I'd never felt the need to compete on the domestic front. Yet now, suddenly, I began arguing irrationally that I, too, was not just good at housework but that I *enjoyed* doing it!

That's how far around the bend I was.

Nevertheless, Jon repeated that he wanted his mother to come.

Big baby, I thought.

Bitch, he no doubt thought.

Steaming, I slammed out of the house and, sitting on the front stoop in the sweltering night, tried to calm myself with a cigarette. It took two, but in the end sanity swept over me. Jon was right. I hated housework. I'd spent *my* life avoiding it. Having Alice in the house would free me to stay longer with Jessica on my hospital visits, would allow me to *play* with the children like I used to. Instead of spending precious hours doing dishes, folding laundry, fixing meals, sweeping, mopping up, I could push Miriam on the backyard swing for as long as her heart desired, let Rachel show me for as much time as she craved the intricacies of the games on her toy computer. We could color together. Maybe even finger-paint if we did it outdoors.

Chastened and conciliatory, I went back into the house and said, "Okay. Call your mother."

"She'll drive us both crazy," Jon averred, temper gone. "She'll ask a million questions. Where does this go? Where does that go? But she'll do anything we ask her to do."

Alice arrived the next day. It turned out that Jon had already, long before our argument, arranged for her to catch an early flight from Phoenix; her coming had never depended on my consent. But I was glad I'd given it. My son-in-law had known far more clearly than I that both of us were in need of relief, in need of getting away at least for a short while from both hospital and household.

After Alice came down, Jon, a "Star Wars" fan, went to see the just-released "Attack of the Clones" and, by mutual agreement, was out of touch for three hours while I stayed at the hospital. That night, he went to the hospital, and I, an aficionado of English country dancing, went to a dance.

It was being held at a college campus far across town. I didn't know a soul in the room. But I knew the dances, with their haunting, melancholic names: "Fain I Would," "Unrequited Love," "Wa' Is Me, Wha' Mun I Do?" I'd been doing English country dancing in New York for years. At the sound of the music—no matter that in New York the music was always live, performed by cellists and pianists, fiddlers and flautists, and here it was coming from a CD player—I hurried to join the long line of dancers. And as we swirled and skipped, weaving in and out in complex patterns to execute dances that had been admired by the very first Queen Elizabeth and passionately beloved by Jane Austen, something in me lifted, let go. I felt not just a diminution of my worries but something more spiritual: a profound and peculiarly calming sense of how insignificant I was, how insignificant we all are, in the grand sweep of history. I've felt this before, felt it when viewing Hadrian's Gate in Turkey, Romanesque churches in France. It's a feeling of transcendence, of rising above one's present circumstances into some other realm. The feeling is paradoxical. Why should a sense of one's inconsequentiality produce psychic ease? I don't know the answer. I just know that it can. That it did for me that night. It hadn't been easy for either Jon or me to give ourselves permission to take these hours of relaxation. But the tonic effect of doing so seemed the equivalent of a week's vacation. We each came back from our mini-adventures revitalized, ready to cope anew. ✍

CHAPTER THREE

New Pathways

THE BRIEF RESPITE WAS FORTUNATE because, as I was learning, recovery from stroke is erratic, a road filled with switchbacks and pitfalls that can cripple the hopeful pilgrims on its path. So much can go wrong. So much that has been going right goes wrong. As May began to slip inexorably toward June, Jessica's heart rate, despite the regulation of her blood volume, continued to be extremely high and her blood pressure extremely low, and the fever she had been running continued to spike. An infectious diseases specialist was brought onto the team, and Jessica was pumped full of antibiotics. Skerhut and Vanover were glum. "We haven't been able to figure out the cause of the fever," Vanover reported toward the end of the Memorial Day weekend. "It could be from some bacteria in Jessica's leg thrombosis. We've ruled out everything else."

"We haven't made any progress since a week ago," Skerhut intoned. "And the longer there's no advancement, the more serious are your daughter's risks from continued bed rest."

He was wearing holiday weekend clothes—jeans and a T-shirt. I'd never seen him in anything but surgical garb before. Maybe he was relaxed because of his casual outfit, or maybe it was because he'd taken most of the day off, but I found him more chatty than usual. Downright revelatory, in fact. He confided to me that when he was in medical school, he'd wanted to be a cosmetic surgeon, but several of his mentors had advised him against it.

"They felt I didn't have the personality for it," he said. "But, in the end, I wasn't too disappointed to give up that goal because, somewhere along the way, I realized that neurosurgery was the most exciting field of surgery there was."

Did I know, he went on to ask me, that one day soon neurosurgeons might be able to determine through brain scans the exact portion of a brain impeding a stroke victim's recovery of motor or speech skills and stimulate that area to work better by using an electrical implant? Did I know that neurosurgeons controlled epileptic seizures in some patients by removing damaged brain tissue or disconnecting one side of the brain from the other, operations being modified and improved upon every year now? "This field is really cutting edge," he quipped.

All too soon, however, Skerhut was back to his grim speculations. "Jessica's clot is dissolving," he said. "But slowly. So there's always the possibility of its breaking apart and a piece going down to her heart or lungs and killing her outright. Or she could have more bleeding, and there's no more room in her brain for bleeding."

I felt as if I was inside *his* brain, where the play of drastic consequences of actions taken or untaken was forever fast forwarding and rewinding. Not a happy place to be.

"The good news," Skerhut allowed then, "is that nothing bad has happened. We just haven't advanced that much."

❦

Marvin Forland and his wife, Ellie, had invited me to dinner that Memorial Day Monday, so when I left the hospital I called my Iranian taxi driver, Dean, and asked him to pick me up. You take your comfort wherever you can get it, and for a while now I'd found myself looking forward to riding with Dean in his cab. I always sat alongside him because my back was beginning to ache and the front seat provided better support. He always offered me a blanket to counter the icy effects of his air-conditioning and always tried to cheer me up. "Don't be despair," he'd say. "Your daughter will be better." He'd distract me with stories about Iranian life in San Antonio. Had I known there were many Iranians in the city? They'd come after the Shah was deposed, started businesses, raised families, built a mosque. "When your daughter is better, I'll show her the mosque."

I'd told Dean that was a very kind offer, and it had set him to making others. "Does she like Iranian food? When she can eat food, I'll ask my wife to prepare something for her. Does she like going out to restaurants? When she can go out to dinner, I'll drive you to one of the Iranian restaurants in town."

When my daughter was better. When she could eat food. When she could go out to dinner. Sometimes as Dean chattered away I could put from my mind how sick Jessica still was, could imagine the scenarios he presented. The IV line disconnected. The drive past a serene mosque. The homemade pilaf and stewed lamb. The Iranian restaurant—crisp white tablecloths, gleaming brass ewers. I'd lose myself in fantasy. This night, however, Dean's certainty, so contrary to what Skerhut had just told me about all that could still go wrong, irritated me.

"Please, Dean," I said. "Jessica's still terribly sick. The doctors keep telling me not to get my hopes up too high."

"Oh, doctors," Dean brushed off my reprimand. "What do they know? They tell you the worst so that you won't sue them. If they told you something good and then it turned out not so good, you might sue."

I hadn't known Dean had a cynical streak—but maybe most people do when it comes to doctors.

"Back home in Iran, people don't sue each other like here," Dean went on.

"We've got more lawyers," I said.

"Veterinarians, too," he commented, which seemed like a non sequitur to me until he added, "I was a veterinarian back home in Iran. That's how I know your daughter will get better."

Bewildered, I turned sideways and looked at him.

"Because people are animals, no? And many times back home in Iran I was called on to look at an animal who out of sudden couldn't move a single limb, who lay down in his stall and couldn't stir even to eat. But one day out of a sudden that animal gets up on its legs, sniffs around and starts to nibble. So will it be with your daughter, *Inshallah*."

Yes, *Inshallah*, I thought, and sank back into the comfort of the car cushion he'd begun bringing along for me.

Dean dropped me at Marvin and Ellie's, and my new friends came to the door and welcomed me inside. The house was beautiful. Decorated with treasures they had gathered on their travels, it was alive with color: the crimsons, rusts and maroons of a rare Berber carpet that hung on the living room wall; the apple greens and cobalt blues of Mexican plates; the smoky grays and opaque blacks of Native American bowls. The hues, so various, so rich, startled me. The hospital was such a bleached-out world, I'd begun to forget how wondrous color could be. But even more startling was how tidy everything looked: the kitchen counters empty of canned goods, jams, condiments; the living room side tables free of newspapers and magazines; the books in the bookcases lined up like West Pointers on parade.

It was a refreshing change from my current living situation. Things were once again chaotic at Jon and Jessica's house. Jon's mother, Alice, had sorted us out for a while, had cooked and frozen some meals, cleaned out the refrigerator, straightened the linen closet, gotten the children to remove their toys from the living room couch and armchairs. She'd taught Rachel how to knit and

Miriam how to play Go Fish, and she'd even trimmed the bangs that had begun to impede my eyesight. But now she'd gone back to Phoenix, and although I could see again, I'd been falling behind on my household duties. Food rotted in the fridge, dust thickened on windowsills and tabletops, and stuffed animals, tousle-haired dolls, tattered chapter books and crayoned drawings had once again taken over the seating areas. Ours was a house without a loving mother. Marvin's house was cared for by the gracious, soft-spoken Ellie, a social worker who had started Child Advocates San Antonio (CASA), the local arm of a national program that recruits, trains and supervises volunteer advocates who find homes and services for children removed by court order from abusive or neglectful families. That night at dinner, Ellie and Marvin, just like Dean, tried to buoy me up. They had a friend, they told me, whose daughter, a medical school student, had had a severe stroke but eventually recovered well enough to continue her studies.

"Don't be discouraged," Ellie said. *Don't be despair.*

"Jessica may improve," Marvin said. *Get up on her legs, sniff around and start to nibble?* "If she can just pull out of this setback."

"If she pulls out, she'll still be paralyzed," I said, refusing to be soothed.

"Yes, but even so, she might be a candidate for rehab. Rehab can work wonders with young stroke victims."

"With young and *paralyzed* stroke victims?" I repeated the frightful word, as if by admitting it to my lexicon, I might be able to come to terms with Jessica's condition.

"Sometimes."

That was the first time any doctor other than an animal doctor had held out to me the possibility that Jessica's paralysis might be ameliorated.

Marvin went on to explain that although for centuries doctors had observed that many stroke victims showed gradual improvement over time, in recent years the medical community had realized improvement could be hastened and recovery made more complete if a patient was given specialized exercises. "Damaged brain cells can't regenerate," he said. "But intact cells can be trained to take on the functions of the damaged cells. That's what rehab attempts to do. Often very successfully."

"In someone as damaged as Jessica?"

"Hard to say. But why not hope?"

⚬⚬⚬

Hope. The very next day Jessica rallied. Her heart rate began coming down, her blood pressure normalized, her fever receded, and Jon was able to make her smile—the first smile I'd seen on her face since before the stroke.

She had a couple of new visitors that day. The first was an outgoing woman who introduced herself as Beth Carpenter. "I'm Jessica's case manager," she said, and cheerfully asked Jessica, "How are you feeling?"

"I'm feeling fine," Jessica replied, which struck me as an odd thing to say, given her condition.

The second new visitor was the chaplain with the tight-lipped, unsmiling mien whom we'd met when Jessica's very survival had seemed so precarious. Surprisingly, this time when he saw Jessica, his face, too, broke into a smile, a wide one, and I saw at once why he had previously kept his mouth so forbiddingly closed. It was riddled with missing teeth, making him look exactly like a Jack-o'-Lantern.

"I'm getting implants," he confessed when he saw me staring and, bearing no grudge for my rudeness, said, "I'm so happy for your daughter." Then, still beaming, he sat down in the chair that faced Jessica and began telling her that he'd been reading *Newsweek* and was worried now, post 9/11, that the civil liberties of Muslims might be curtailed. "That would be wrong," he said. "So wrong, don't you think?"

"Yes, wrong," Jessica iterated, listening with what appeared to be real interest and comprehension.

The chaplain worried some more over the state of the American body politic, then got up to go, giving out a hearty, "Goodbye, and God bless you."

"God bless you, too," Jessica responded.

Her words that afternoon were not just audible but oddly formal.

Such formality, said my neuropsychologist husband when I spoke to him later that day, was indicative of a phenomenon not uncommon among poststroke patients. "It's a form of echolalia," Max explained. "After a stroke, survivors are still in a confused world. They have to repeat the words of others in order to frame responses. We call it language that isn't flexible."

I preferred my own explanation: Jessica was taking cues about what to say by listening to and understanding the conversation of those around her.

It was a subtle difference, but to me a significant one.

Better yet, on my return visit to the hospital that evening, I noticed that she was beginning to regain flexible language—to use her own words to comment on things she noticed. As I stood up from my bedside chair and made ready to leave for the night, she said something that sounded like gibberish to me. "One of your associates is leaving, too," she said.

My associates? Had she forgotten who I was? Mistaken me for one of her doctors? I blurted out, "What? What associates?" and she replied, "A person of your own age." She was staring at a spot over my shoulder.

I turned around and looked behind me. A woman who appeared to be, like me, in her sixties, was passing outside Jessica's cubicle on her way to the nurses' station. Jessica's brain had registered a similarity between me and the stranger outside, and she had come up with the thought that given our similarity we must be connected in some way. Associated. This was incorrect word use, but it had its positive side: not only was Jessica groping to express a convoluted idea, but she was noting something going on beyond her hospital bed, in the more distant environment.

The next day the doctors started talking about moving Jessica out of the ICU.

They had kept her there as long as possible, Dr. Vanover explained, but the cost of continuing to do so was formidable. "We're going to have to transfer her to a ward with fewer nurses per patient. And if she remains medically stable in that setting, she'll soon have to be moved out of the hospital altogether."

Still high on the signs of progress I'd observed in my daughter, not to mention the conversation I'd had with Marvin the night of the dinner at his house, I assumed Vanover meant that Jessica would be moved out of the hospital into a rehabilitation clinic. Indeed, a social worker from such a clinic had stopped by earlier in the day to interview her. She'd been asleep when he arrived, and after promising to return another time, he'd spent a good 15 minutes telling me how exceptional his clinic was at helping the brain develop what he called "new neural pathways."

I mentioned the social worker's spiel to Vanover, but he shook his head. "Jessica may not be a candidate for rehabilitation," he cautioned me. "Yes, the swelling in her brain has gone down, but that's not the crucial factor now. Most of Jessica's impairment has been caused by the hemorrhage, not the swelling, and the hemorrhage has probably completely destroyed some areas of her brain."

"What about the brain finding new pathways?" I blurted out.

"Well, yes, it can. But it takes time before those pathways can develop."

"But doesn't rehab speed that development along?" I was a mini-expert by now.

"It can," he nodded. "But not everyone can handle rehab. Jessica may need to go to an SNF. A skilled nursing facility."

I didn't like the sound of it. A nursing facility. That's where they store the hopeless and the aged, I thought. That's a home, a nursing home, whatever fancy name they give it. How would Jessica ever improve if she was in a nursing home?

"Why?" I pleaded. "Why can't she go to a rehab place?"

"They may feel she's too damaged to benefit from their facilities. They may not want her."

I had the oddest recollection then. I remembered when Jessica's father and I were trying to get Jessica, a precocious three-year-old, into a Manhattan nursery school: the stressful "interviews"; the noncommittal interviewers; the jockeying among fellow parents; the very preposterousness of having three-year-olds compete for an academic placement.

"Of course, you and Jon should look at some rehab clinics," Vanover broke into my thoughts. "But you'll have to look at some SNFs, too."

I was hardly paying attention. I was back in a nursery school on West End Avenue in New York City, where a dour headmistress was showing Jessica the lid of a tin of chocolates stamped with a photograph of Queen Elizabeth at her coronation. "What's this?" the headmistress asked.

"A queen," my little girl promptly replied.

"No, a *picture* of a queen," the headmistress said sourly.

It had been one of many such irritating encounters. But we'd managed. No. Jessica had managed. She'd won over every interviewer whose job it was to winnow a school's list of applicants. She'll do it again, I told myself, not quite believing it but needing to believe it. Somehow, she'll do it again. She's got to do it again.

❦

The following morning, Beth Carpenter met with us and gave us a list of places to visit—both SNFs and rehab clinics. Marvin, too, recommended a rehab clinic. Apparently, there was some need for a speedy decision on our part—not between a rehab clinic and an SNF, but about which rehab clinic or SNF. The doctors would decide, based on Jessica's progress over the next couple of days, what kind of facility it would be. In the meantime, Beth advised, Jon and

I ought to visit a couple of places in each of the two categories. "That way, once Jessica is ready to be transferred out of the hospital, you'll be able to indicate which clinic or nursing facility you want her sent to," she said. "Not that it's entirely up to you. The institutions themselves have to decide if they think a prospective patient can be helped by what they have to offer. Still, assuming more than one place feels it can help Jessica, we'd like to transfer her to a place you prefer."

Prefer? What were we to look for? What criteria should we use when making a choice? Jon and I, like most people who are asked to make a decision about post-hospital placement for a family member who's had a stroke, were clueless.

"You should think about things like how far the place is from your home," Beth instructed, handing each of us a printed sheet of paper. "How easy will it be for you to visit? And you should ask the director to show you around. Have a look at the gym. The patients' rooms. The dining facilities."

"What about a facility's reputation?" Jon asked. "Shouldn't we look into that?"

Beth shook her head. "You can if you want, but it's really not necessary," she said. "These places all have good reputations. We wouldn't have them on our list if they didn't."

Reassured, Jon and I looked the list over carefully, making check marks alongside the ones nearest to the family's house. But when I got to the bottom of the list I realized that the place Marvin had recommended wasn't on the sheet Beth had handed us.

"What about Reeves?" I asked Beth. "Over at University Hospital. Marvin Forland told us about it."

"I'm not familiar with that one," the case manager replied with a puzzled expression on her compassionate face. "It may be new. Or it could be highly selective about the patients it takes. But I suppose that if Dr. Forland suggested the place, it's probably okay."

"What *makes* a place okay?" I asked. "I mean, can we find out which facilities have the most successful programs?"

"You can ask for outcome data," Beth sighed, "but the data will be more or less meaningless. One place could consistently have more successful outcomes than another place. But that might be because it only accepts less incapacitated patients. Or younger patients—they generally recover more swiftly and fully than older patients."

Beth was trying her best to help us, but it was clear that her job required her to avoid touting one place over another. We would be flying blind.

Determined to cover as much ground as we could, we set out, Beth's list and a city map in hand. The first facility we visited was a large rehabilitation center that overlooked a vast parking lot. Shepherded by a guide, we saw the facility's two-to-a-room patient quarters—they had a view of the parking lot's sea of painted metal and glittery chrome—and toured viewless corridors. As we traversed them, our guide pointed out gyms, dining rooms, and visitors' lounges, but he never took us inside any of these areas.

The second place we visited was also a rehabilitation facility. Smaller than the first, its patient quarters, also two-to-a-room, overlooked green lawns with splashing fountains. Our guide allowed us access to a gym where, rude intruders on patient privacy, we stood in a corner and observed a large assemblage of patients using exercise equipment under the direction of a handful of physiotherapists. We were also allowed access to a large dining room where, before our guide whisked us away, we noticed several paralyzed patients sitting helplessly before trays of rapidly cooling food, nary a staff member in sight to feed them.

The third place was an SNF. It was even drearier than I had imagined it would be. Its floors were made of gray concrete, the kind with drains that allow for easy flushing with water. Its patient rooms were four-bed wards. There was no one in the establishment's tiny gym, not a patient or a therapist. And the patients we saw in their rooms all looked desperately sick. "Like they're dying," Jon murmured to me. "Not like they're recovering."

Afterward, we drove to Reeves, the clinic Marvin had recommended. Located on a single floor at San Antonio's large University Hospital, it specialized in treating people with spinal cord damage and brain injuries and only had room for 25 patients. Each brain-injured patient was housed in his or her own room because, our guide explained to us, "the brain-injured shouldn't be exposed to too much stimulation, and when rooms are shared there's always too much going on." The rooms were spartan, but they had a comforting look, like hotel rooms in an unfamiliar city.

Reeves' small gym had glass walls adorned with homey lace curtains, so it was easy for us to stand in the corridor and observe the activity within: therapists, sometimes two or three to a patient, supervising mat and machine exercises. The patients, Jon pointed out to me as we gazed through the glass walls, looked younger than those we'd seen at the other facilities. "More likely," he said wistfully, quoting what Beth Carpenter had told us the day before about younger patients, "to recover more swiftly."

The clinic had numerous grace notes: a little kitchen where patients could be instructed in simple but lost culinary skills; a technology room for teaching them their lost computer skills; a small dining room decorated with plants and colorful posters; a lounge for both patients and visitors fitted out with couches, a piano, bookshelves stacked with board games, and a blackboard with chalks.

There was also a room our guide called the "real world" room. Equipped with a double bed, a bathroom, a kitchenette, and a dining area, it was set up like a small private residence. "This is where all our patients stay, accompanied by a family member, the night before they go home," the guide explained, "so they can practice what it'll be like to be in the outside world again."

I fell in love with Reeves because of that room. Seeing it sent me whirling into fantasy once again, conjuring up visions of Jessica staying there with Jon one day, watching TV with him not from her bed but on the puffy couch, sharing sleeping quarters, fixing toast and eggs in the little kitchenette. Jon fell in love with Reeves because of the young patients he'd so wistfully noticed in the gym, and because of the lounge with its piano and board games and blackboard. He felt the girls wouldn't be frightened by the place, might even enjoy visiting their mother in such a setting. "It looks," he whispered to me, "sort of like an after-school day care center."

∞

Every day that followed our tour brought signs that Jessica's brain was less damaged than her doctors had predicted it would be. At night, after the children had gone to bed, Jon and I would exchange word of marvels each of us had witnessed.

Me: "She moved her left thumb. I saw it!"

Jon: "She moved her left forefinger. I saw it and so did Marvin."

Like the parents of infants, who view even the tiniest developmental accomplishment as cause for elation, we crowed over every change in Jessica, dwelling on it, recounting it over and over to each other—and often recounting it yet again to family members and friends who telephoned.

Me: "She can swallow! They're giving her ice!"

As preparation for moving Jessica out of the hospital, her intravenous line had been disconnected and a feeding tube inserted into her stomach, but despite the hydration she was receiving through the tube, she'd complained of feeling dry-mouthed, and her nurses had begun satisfying her thirst with tiny slivers of ice.

Jon: "When I came there tonight she was singing!"

The night nurse had put the cassette player Jon had given Jessica on her pillow and placed the earphones in her ears, and when Jon walked in she was singing aloud along with Ella Fitzgerald. "I love Paris in the springtime," she was crooning. "I love Paris in the fall."

Such daily improvements in Jessica had a palliative effect on the back pain I'd been feeling. Stress had been making that pain worse and worse, had been making me feel at times that I could hardly walk. But now, when I got into bed at night, I recited Jon's observations, reviewed my own, recited his again, and felt my backache diminish.

This was only one of my bedtime rituals. Just before I fell off to sleep, I invariably said a kind of prayer, which went like this: "Please, Whoever or Whatever controls this universe, please don't let Jessica get sent to a nursing home." Back on the East Coast, my friend Fran offered up this prayer for me in her synagogue on Madison Avenue; my friend Elizabeth, in her Episcopalian church on Fifth Avenue; my friend Alfred, in his Catholic church on 82nd Street; my friend Sheila, in her Evangelical Church in Brooklyn; my friend David, in his Quaker Meeting Hall in Philadelphia. Other friends in other places were also praying: my friend Kitsi to Buddha; Sylvia, to Brahma and Vishnu; and Dean, to Allah. I often drifted off to sleep counting deities.

But pretty soon it occurred to me that some human intervention might be in order. Jessica's doctors had decided that she was a candidate for rehab—provided some clinic was willing to take her. Two of the rehab clinics we'd visited had said, yes, they were willing. But Reeves had turned her down. A member of its medical staff, we were later to learn, had deemed Jessica's case hopeless.

Jon got depressed. He'd had visions of strolling hand-in-hand with the girls into Reeves' child-friendly lounge. I was miserable. I'd seen the devotion of the clinic's physical therapists. I'd seen the kitchen where occupational therapists taught the forgotten intricacies of lighting an oven and boiling water, the computer room where they reminded patients how to do email and Google search. Above all, I'd seen the "real world" room.

Not happy with what I was about to do, I made up my mind to approach Marvin for help. I'd always been high-minded and judgmental about people who pulled strings to get advantages not obtainable by the less well connected. A much-loved friend of mine with powerful political friends had pulled strings when, on the verge of heart failure and in need of a human heart valve, she'd called in favors, asking her political connections to try to get her to the top of the waiting list. Her efforts worked, she got the valve, and while it meant she would live and I would have my dear friend for longer, there were times I couldn't help wondering about the person who'd originally been first in line, the unknown someone who might have sickened or died after being supplanted.

But scruples be damned. For my child, I would throw them to the wind. Not for myself, but for my child I could, and would, do anything.

I'm sure this must be a universal feeling. "For my daughter's sake, I can be anything—brave, strong, fearless," a Hindu housekeeper thinks to herself in Thrity Umrigar's novel *The Space Between Us.* "For her sake, I can walk on crushed glass, lie down on hot coals, walk through ice-cold waters." For *my* daughter's sake I merely had to swallow principles.

It was going to be a difficult gulp. Kind as he was, Marvin wasn't an easy sort of man to ask for help; he was so reserved and dignified that applying to him for a favor seemed almost beyond the bounds of propriety. Nevertheless, I swallowed hard, called Marvin at home, and begged him to intercede for us at Reeves.

"It's not up to me," Marvin rejected my entreaty. "The doctors at Reeves make their own decisions."

"Still, surely you can do something!" I pleaded. "You've seen how much Jessica's coming along. You've seen how hard she's trying."

Marvin sighed. "It wouldn't be right to question my colleagues."

∞

Marvin's response to my entreaties had been so discouraging that I felt myself slipping into my old despair and worrying obsessively about the children. Were they all right? Were they really all right?

Beth Carpenter, Jessica's case manager, was worried about them, too. Rachel and Miriam hadn't seen their mother in weeks because children weren't permitted in the intensive care unit, and according to Beth this was exceedingly unfortunate, because it was imperative to children's mental health that they be allowed to see a sick parent. "Children sometimes think," Beth said, "that people are lying to them when they say a hospitalized parent is just sick, and they secretly believe the parent is actually dead." She offered to try to get the rules prohibiting children in the ICU waived so that Rachel and Miriam could have a brief visit with their mother.

The idea made me uncomfortable. The ICU was a terrifying place. The curtains around patients' beds were rarely drawn, and if you weren't careful where you let your eyes roam, you caught glimpses of bleeding bodies, writhing bodies, the moribund and even the newly expired. Jessica, too, was a frightening sight. She was still laced with tubes, her face was gaunt, she couldn't move her limbs, and her head remained turned to the right side, so that she couldn't see anyone who wasn't directly in her line of vision. Vanover told me her doctors didn't know whether she couldn't turn her head because her neck muscles were temporarily frozen or because the part of her brain that controlled neck movement had been irreparably damaged. If the children visited, they'd be seeing not their mother, but the carapace of a mother.

But Jon agreed with Beth, who promised she'd get the ICU staff to draw the curtains around the other patients' beds. "It'll be great for Jessica to see the kids," Jon told me. "And it's got to be better for the kids to see her than to not see her. Because maybe they do think I've been lying to them and Jessica is really dead. But even if that's not the case, Jessica's their mother. If this is how she is, how she looks, if she's going to be paralyzed the rest of her life, she's still their mother, and they've got to get used to it and accept her as she is."

❦

Rachel wrote a story for her mother, Miriam drew a picture, both girls allowed me to brush their hair without their usual shrieks of protest, and on a Saturday morning, Jon drove us all to the hospital. I was still uneasy. More uneasy. The girls seemed nervous. They chattered incessantly in the car and, when we asked them to stop, sang verse after verse of "The Bear Went Over the Mountain" until we had to tell them to stop that, too. Jon had warned them that Jessica was still very sick and that she would look different and might not be in the mood to talk much. But how would they take it when they actually saw her? It was one thing to be forewarned, another to experience their mother's condition.

As we walked down the long corridors of the hospital, Miriam's nervousness translated into hijinks. She wouldn't keep pace with the rest of us, instead racing about on her chubby little legs and running circles around Rachel. Her big sister became annoyed, then motherly, catching up with Miriam and trying to distract her by pointing out details in the photographs that adorned the corridors' walls. At the entrance to the intensive care unit, however, both children turned serious and silent.

A nurse led the way to Jessica's cubicle, and, indeed, it was the only one in which the curtain was pulled aside and a figure lying on a bed was visible. All the other cubicles were curtained off, just as Beth had promised.

Miriam rushed into the cubicle, calling out, "Mommy! Mommy!" and begged unsuccessfully to be lifted up onto the bed so she could hug her mother. Rachel, still restrained, stood back, clutching her father's hand, until, after a few moments, she walked gingerly to stand where Jessica's face was turned and ceremoniously held up before her mother's eyes a hand-drawn Get Well card. Less responsive than she'd been the day before, Jessica looked at it but didn't speak. Then, shifting her glance from the card to Rachel herself, she stared wordlessly into Rachel's eyes. Miriam pushed forward, planting herself in front of her sister and waving her drawing around. It was a rendition of a tree in full bloom, its branches sporting flowers crayoned in crimson and cerise and magenta, intoxicating Crayola colors that delighted the three-year-old. Miriam swung it in the air and then suddenly stopped, distracted by a bag of pink fluid still hanging on Jessica's disconnected intravenous pole. Dropping the drawing, she shot a plump little arm in the pole's direction. "What's that?" she asked, pointing at the dangling bag.

"It's yogurt," Jessica said.

Yogurt! Jessica hadn't just spoken; she'd tried to make a joke. Jon and I laughed, Rachel joined in, and although Miriam didn't quite get why we were laughing, she giggled, too, and asked once again to be lifted onto the bed. "I want to hug Mommy," she declared.

Jon picked her up and let her put her arms around the motionless Jessica.

"I want to hug Mommy, too," Rachel clamored.

"Why don't you hold Mommy's hand instead," Jon deflected her—Rachel, at eight, wouldn't be easy to lift and hold just so over her mother.

"Okay," Rachel agreed, and took hold of Jessica's right hand. But Jessica's grasp was limp, and Rachel quickly withdrew her fingers, saying, "It's time for my story. I want to read Mommy my story." With that, she extricated from her jacket pocket a few sheets of lined yellow paper and began reading. "Angela was an enchanted person," she intoned. "An angel."

An angel? Our family rarely mentioned angels, except for the one that came at Passover and sipped the Seder wine, but angels were much talked about in Texas. Had one of Rachel's teachers told her that if her mother died she would go up to heaven and become an angel? I listened in alarm as Rachel went on, "All Angela could write was English. Then she went to Angel School and got a book on how to write Anglish, the angel language." Ah, so it was going to be humorous! I felt relieved. "That language was very hard," Rachel continued. "Angela practiced night and day because she wanted to write a story. So she learned the whole alphabet, and after a while she wrote the story of Clyde the Cloud."

At this point, the story began detailing the picaresque adventures of Clyde, but I don't remember much of the rest except that it was indeed funny, with Clyde forever bumping into his fellow

clouds and causing havoc—and rain. I was too anxious to con-
centrate on the specifics of Clyde's encounters, too bent on hoping that Jessica would interrupt the account at some point, react,
say something. Which at last she did, but only when Rachel pro-
nounced, "The End."

Jessica responded to this cue, but her tone was so soft it was
itself like a cloud. "Thank you," she said with that formality I had
noticed previously. "Thank you so much."

Rachel seemed disappointed. I think that, despite all the warn-
ings issued by her father and me, she'd been expecting her mother
to utter her familiar, "That's really good, honey," or even, "Wow,
that was cool!"

We didn't stay long after that. Jon sent the three of us out to
the lounge area and remained with his wife for a while. Then he
took the girls home, while I lingered at the hospital, hoping to
spend some more time with Jessica, who'd fallen asleep.

I was there, still, when she awakened from her nap, her eyes slowly opening and spotting me in the chair on the right side of the bed.

"Oh, Jessica, you saw the girls!" I chattered. "Remember? Remember?"

"Of course. How could I not?" she answered slowly, more responsive now than she had been earlier.

I went on to ask whether she'd found the visit good, and she
replied in perfect syntax, "How could it not have been?" But she
was still sleepy, and moments later her eyes closed again.

I sat outside in the lounge area and napped myself. So I didn't
see Marvin come into the lounge and make his way to Jessica's cubicle. It was only when he exited that I noticed him. "I've just had
a wonderful conversation with your daughter," he announced,
thoroughly startling me.

"A conversation?"

"Yes, a real back and forth. I asked her how the visit with the
girls had gone. She said, 'Beautifully'—she's a great grammarian,
don't you think?—and then I asked her about what she used to do

on her job, and she told me about writing political papers and attending council meetings."

I felt a bit jealous. Clearly, Jon, the girls and I had come at the wrong moment in the alternating cycles of exhaustion and alertness produced by brain injury.

Those cycles are unpredictable. Patients have not just good days and bad days. They have good hours and bad hours, good minutes and bad minutes. That's the way it is with strokes.

And this is how it is with children: they're full of surprises. The next day, the girls woke up and demanded that Jon take them to see their mother again. They hadn't been put off by her condition. Or, if they had been, overnight they'd processed what they'd seen and, just as Jon had predicted, accepted their mother the way she was.

They went to the hospital several times during the next few days, days during which Jessica was moved from the ICU into the step-down unit and given what was surely the most important test she'd ever had to take in her life—the examination the hospital called "the swallow test."

Happily, she aced it, and afterward the technician who administered the test wrote on Jessica's chart, "Pureed food OK." Also, "Pleasure food." That meant, I was informed by a nurse, mashed potatoes and even ice cream. I tried to imagine what it must feel like to eat ice cream as if for the first time, experience anew its velvety coldness and syrupy sweetness, but my imagination wasn't up to the task.

During Jessica's time in the step-down unit, Marvin had frequent conversations with her on all manner of subjects—of all of us, he seemed the most able to draw my daughter out. He talked to her about poetry, he reported to me, and Judaism and birthday parties and child rearing. And on Jessica's fourth day in the unit, he suggested to us that we ask Reeves to reevaluate her.

We did. Reeves reexamined her by now voluminous records and debated her recent progress at what we later learned was a highly disputatious staff meeting, with the physician who'd earlier declared her case hopeless still doubting she could be helped. But the rest of the staff was more optimistic, and in the end Reeves Rehabilitation Center agreed to take my still-paralyzed daughter into their care.

I thought that perhaps Marvin had intervened on our behalf, maybe uttered a positive word or two into the right ears. But when, intending to thank him, I mentioned this speculation, Marvin shook his head. "I had nothing to do with it," he said. "It was all Jessica's doing."

PART TWO

THE LONG ROAD BACK

Chapter Four

Trapped

"WE GOT MOMMY BACK," Miriam said to me over the phone a few days after Jessica entered Reeves. "But not regular Mommy."

I'd returned to New York because my husband was there. Because my friends were there. Because I'd been working on the *Chapman* book when Jessica got sick and the manuscript was due shortly.

All the weeks of not writing had given me the feeling that I'd never be able to finish *Chapman*, that my inspiration had dried up. Words and ideas are malleable, like clay, but as with clay you can't leave words and ideas alone for too long. If you do, they harden, become desiccated.

I needed to get back to work. But I couldn't. The book was so linked to Jessica. I'd chosen its subject, a scandalous 19th-century murder case, because Jessica had asked me not to embark on another book like those I'd been doing the previous few years. Those were contemporary true-crime books, works that involved investigative research with living subjects, as opposed to historical research with long-dead protagonists. The last one had put me in a certain amount of danger. I'd had to travel alone to Argentina, where the central figure—a drug dealer and serial killer who'd been the suspect in the murder of a friend of mine—had grown up, in order to interview his family and get to know his habits and haunts. Later, when I had interviewed him in prison, he'd warned me to be careful what I said about him. "I got people on the outside," he'd said. "You betta watch out."

"Mom, please don't do that kind of book any more," Jessica, concerned for my safety, had said. "Why don't you do something historical for a change?" And I had taken her up on the suggestion.

She'd been an integral part of my writing life ever since she was a child. Back in the 1970s, when I used to review restaurants for *New York* magazine, I would often take her along to dinner with Max and me if the place I was doing was one where attentiveness to children needed to be considered. She was so young then that she'd sometimes grow restless, so if the meal took a long time, I'd assign her to check out the bathroom facilities. She would take notes, writing on a pad in big childish script what she thought of the decor and the plumbing, and I'd try to include her observations in my pieces. When she entered high school and I was working on a novel, she and I used to act out the physical gestures involved in a scene—the precise way an arm might be raised in a quarrel, the exact posture a character breaking up with a lover might manifest. As she got older, we talked about the ideas behind the books I was working on—the personalities of the protagonists, the best sequencing of material, the grammatical structure of a sentence, the song and rhythm of a paragraph. I couldn't write while Jessica's life hung in the balance.

There was a lot else I couldn't do. I couldn't get out of bed for hours in the mornings. I couldn't eat. I couldn't make love to my husband.

All I wanted to do was sleep. When I slept, Jessica came back to me, animated and energetic. But when I woke, I had to learn the diminution of her all over again.

I had Jessica back, but not regular Jessica.

Every evening I received a phone call from Jon. There was good news. Jessica was beginning to be able to use her right arm and hold onto things in her right hand, and the muscles in her left arm had relaxed enough to allow her to move the arm and hand not just from her midline to her face but even down to her thigh. Then there was bad news. The muscles in that arm had gone into spasm, and the arm had bent and become frozen across her chest like a bandolier. She couldn't get it to straighten down at all.

Still, one evening Jon reported, "Today they got her dressed and into a wheelchair. They use a crane to lift her out of bed and into the chair."

"How'd that go?"

"So-so. She's scared of the crane, thinks they'll drop her."

"Could they?" I was as scared as she must have been. A fall is one of the most dreaded things that can happen to a paralyzed patient. Broken bones add insult to immobility.

"She can't fall," Jon reassured me. "Two nurses operate the device. They put a kind of hammock thing under her while she's in bed, strap her into it, and swing her up and into the wheelchair. Then they strap her into the chair so she doesn't topple over."

Another evening: "She had lunch in the dining room. Sitting in the wheelchair."

"How'd that go?"

"Pretty good. She liked the nurse who fed her."

Then one evening: "She's cracking jokes."

"Jokes? Really?"

"Really. The nurse who was feeding her said she was on a seafood diet, and Jess came out with that old one, 'Yes, me too. I see food and I eat it.'"

I laughed. Sounded good. But whenever I asked, "Can she turn her head?" there'd be a pause, and then, "No."

❦

Marvin called me, too. He no longer paid Jessica regular visits, perhaps because University Hospital was a longer drive for him than Northeast Baptist had been. Or perhaps it was out of deference to the staff at Reeves—knowing him, I suspected he didn't want the physical therapists to think he was looking over their shoulders. Whatever the reason, he kept up with Jessica's progress, or lack of it, by talking to his medical colleagues. "They're getting Jessica a new wheelchair," he told me one day. "A chair that will support her head. It'll make a big difference. Give her some confidence."

"They're considering using Botox for her neck and the frozen left arm," he said another time.

I knew about Botox. Several friends had had it injected into the wrinkles between their eyes. Made from the same toxin that causes botulism, the acute food poisoning that results in sometimes deadly paralysis, the substance makes wrinkles less prominent by paralyzing tiny facial muscles, causing them to loosen their grip on facial skin.

"It's a new treatment for stroke patients," Marvin explained. "Experimental. The toxin has to be very carefully placed in exactly the right muscle."

"Jeez, the treatment," I said, "sounds worse than what it's treating."

"Not if it's done right," Marvin said. "Lei Zhang, the head of medical services on the unit, is very experienced."

❦

Jessica herself even spoke with me on the phone. For her to do this, a nurse had to dial my number and then position the phone near where Jessica's head was turned and have her support the phone with her right hand.

One time she told me that she liked the rehab center. Another time, that she'd been placed on a tilt table, a device that can move a prone patient into an upright position.

"I was afraid," Jessica confessed. And then, "I passed out."

"Oh, baby!" I gasped. "How awful."

"It's okay, Mom," she replied, in the calmest of tones. "It's an expected reaction after someone's been lying down for so long."

She may have been calm, but I wasn't. I'd grow particularly uneasy when the nurse who set Jessica up with the phone left the room while we were talking and the phone would slip out of Jessica's hand. I'd try to say something she could hear or hear *her* say something, all to no avail. She couldn't retrieve the phone, and after a while the phone would go dead. We'd be out of communication until I called the nurses' station and asked whoever answered to go into Jessica's room, hang up her phone, and dial me again.

❧

I was on the phone a lot those days, not just down to Texas but with friends in New York. "She's alive!" they'd say with evangelical fervor. Or, "I'm sure she'll get better." My irritability grew with each well-meaning call. What was so great about being alive but paralyzed? How could anyone be sure she'd get better when her doctors themselves weren't sure? I reacted worst to the friend who insisted I ought to bring Jessica to New York because, she asserted, "Here's where the best rehab facilities are." Didn't she understand that Jessica had a family in Texas? Besides, who *said* the best rehab places were in New York? I understood that my friends were trying to help, but repeatedly I would succumb to anger over provincial or innocent remarks. I didn't, I realized, want to talk to anyone except Jessica—and to attempt communicating with her over the phone was merely to court frustration. I needed to talk to her in person, needed to be with her. After two weeks in New York, I packed up my manuscript and research files, kissed Max goodbye, and flew back to Texas.

Arriving in San Antonio on a summer's night is like stepping into a sauna: the limb-binding air isn't just hot but profoundly humid. Waiting in the terminal for their luggage and anticipating the damp, heavy air just outside the doors, my fellow passengers were shedding clothes—a jacket here, a long-sleeved shirt there. I too shed a shirt and, after getting my bags, trudged outside to the taxi line, where I saw to my astonishment that Dean's taxi was three cars down in the line.

"Dean!" I called out, waving an arm excitedly. Braving a cacophony of car horns and curses, Dean pulled ahead to where I stood and yelled out his window, "You're back!" It's an omen, I thought. A good omen. There must be, what, a thousand taxi drivers in San Antonio? More? But here was Dean, out looking for a fare so late on this hot night. We greeted each other like friends. Like family.

"How's your daughter?" he asked, jumping out of the cab and, remembering my bad back, opening the front passenger door for me.

"She can sit up in a wheelchair," I boasted.

"Told you," he said. "Only with a horse it's standing up. Because they can't sit. Except sometimes. In the circus."

I laughed, and he hefted my bags into the trunk. But I clutched the computer. *Chapman* was in there. Ready to go to the publisher if I could just get back to work and finish the last chapter.

It was well after midnight when Dean's cab arrived in front of Jon and Jessica's home. Eyelids drooping, Jon opened the door and, Texas style, I hurried from the air-conditioned car into the air-conditioned house, tripping as I went over Rachel's toy computer and a scattering of Miriam's toy food. Plastic onions and broccoli. Oranges. Cucumbers. Cookies. Inedible, but only a year or two ago much mouthed. I'd get the fake food off the floor tomorrow. I was where I needed to be.

When I saw Jessica the next morning, she was indeed sitting up, her torso strapped into her wheelchair so she wouldn't topple over. It was a gigantic chair, the chair Marvin had told me about, high enough to support her still-paralyzed neck, and she was wearing clothes, real clothes: jeans and a long-sleeved T-shirt. I hadn't seen her in anything but a hospital gown in so long that I memorized every bit of her apparel. The striped socks. Her old sneakers with their gone-to-gray laces. The white T-shirt with its pattern of red medallions I'd given her a few years ago. She looked pale and exceedingly thin. But her dark, thick-lashed eyes were bright. And her newly shampooed hair was brushed and glistening. "You look beautiful," I told her.

"That's thanks to my hair stylist, Mr. Norman," she said.

Her hair stylist? Had she imagined she'd gone out of the hospital, visited her beauty salon?

She smiled at the perplexed look on my face. "My hair stylist," she repeated, pointing to a male nurse out in the corridor. "Norman," she called, "Come meet my mother."

I met Norman and a phalanx of others involved in Jessica's care that day. Her physiotherapists, Beth Schlegel, Mariam Hammerle and Neha Shah. Her speech therapist, Kathy Thompson. Her recreational therapist, Dawn Preston. Her occupational therapist, Will Schalla.

The head of the entire inpatient therapy unit, Will had taught high school English and theater arts before deciding to become a physiotherapist. Handsome, with long limbs and a trim Van Dyke beard, he was Jessica's favorite. "We're hoping," he told me in a gentle West Texas drawl, "that we'll be able to get your daughter's frozen arm to regain mobility." To do so, he explained, a technique called serial casting would be employed. This procedure involved putting a cast on the arm and each day altering the cast so that it pulled the arm downward by incremental degrees. Once the arm's position began its descent, however minuscule, the limb could be stretched little by little to increase its mobility. However, in order to loosen the locked muscles sufficiently to make it possible to put on a cast—in order to get what Will, grinning, called a "foothold" on the arm—it would be helpful if Jessica could receive a Botox injection.

Botox was expensive. One vial of the precious toxin, I discovered, cost between four hundred and five hundred dollars, and some patients required as many as eight vials. At the time of Jessica's stroke, the medication had not yet been approved for use with stroke patients by the Food and Drug Administration. Consequently, insurance companies were reluctant to pay for it, and very few stroke patients who could have benefited from Botox were being given the toxin. Eventually, as scientific evidence of its effectiveness continued to mount, some insurers began reimbursing for these treatments, but it would be another eight years before the FDA approved Botox for this use.

⸲⸲⸲

Will was optimistic about Jessica's potential for recovery. So were her other therapists. The field of rehabilitation attracts positive-thinking individuals, people with not just a keen desire to help others but also a willingness to measure success by teaspoonfuls. "In most other medical disciplines," Reeves's medical director, Dr. John King, was one day to tell me, "you see results quickly. The patient either gets better, or dies. It's different in rehab. We look for two things when we're staffing. People who can tolerate delayed gratification, and people with encouraging, upbeat personalities."

The staff at the clinic fit that bill, with one notable exception. The highly touted Dr. Zhang was far from upbeat. "Your daughter has had so much brain damage," he told me when I encountered him in a corridor outside Jessica's room soon after meeting Will, "she may never regain the use of her immobilized limbs. Or be able to turn her neck."

"What about Botox?" I interrupted. "I heard Botox was being considered."

"It's a very costly treatment," Zhang replied in a clipped cheerless voice. "The FDA hasn't given its go-ahead for cases like your daughter's. The insurance company may not pay."

Talking to Zhang was like being pummeled. "Your daughter," he went on to say, "most likely won't be here with us much longer. The insurance company has approved her for only one week."

"I know," I said. It was—and still is—standard practice among insurance companies to pay for inpatient rehabilitation on a week-by-week basis, extending coverage only if a patient shows progress. No progress, no insurance coverage. Patients are sent home or to nursing facilities.

"Jessica's making progress," I insisted to Zhang.

"Slow progress," he responded in a dreary tone. "Very slow."

Zhang, I thought, as he disappeared down the corridor, must be the person on the staff who had deemed Jessica's case hopeless. And now he wants to be right.

I walked slowly back to Jessica's room, arriving just as she was being hoisted back into her bed by Norman and another nurse. She was letting out a yelp of fear as they swung her in the air, midway between chair and bed. She'd never liked heights of any sort. Nor had Joe, her father. Acrophobic, he'd panicked on one of our first dates because our opera tickets were at the very top of the Metropolitan Opera House's topmost tier. Years later Max had told me the phobia was genetic. Max, who'd been a pioneer in the genetic causes of schizophrenia, was always surprising me with information about the many things that could be passed from parent to child. It was he who'd first told me and Jessica about the heritability of shyness, information that had helped Jessica enormously in those days she'd been wrestling with diffidence, because it had enabled her to stop viewing the trait as some kind of personal failure.

Jessica had inherited so many things from her biological father. She had Joe's acrophobia. His stunning, dense eyebrows. His height. His sardonic wit. And Joe, too, had had a blood clot. In his intestine.

We'd been newlyweds, kids so young it hadn't occurred to us to buy health insurance. Two years after our wedding, Joe developed a pain in his abdomen so severe it made him wail in anguish both before and after heavy doses of painkillers. When the pain became unbearable, we went to a hospital emergency room. The staff there decided that, since he was a young man, the cause of his pain was probably appendicitis. Those were the days before magnetic resonance imaging, before doctors could see into their patients' innards without opening them up surgically and having a look at what was happening inside. Joe was rushed to surgery, and his appendix was removed. But soon after the anesthesia wore off, he began complaining of pain, and shortly he was screaming again.

"I see your husband is an editor," a young intern rifling through Joe's chart said to me. "A writer and an editor. Does he ever make up stories?"

Was he implying Joe's pain was imaginary, a fantasy? Listening to my husband scream, I was infuriated by this dismissive intern, and that night Joe's parents and I called in a renowned abdominal surgeon. Without scans, the surgeon had no definite idea what was causing the still steadily increasing pain. All he knew was that there was something terribly awry somewhere in Joe's gut. "It's exploratory surgery," he said to Joe's father. Who said to me, "Like looking, you know, for the source of the Nile."

Once the surgeon opened the abdomen of my poor young husband, he quickly enough found the source of the pain: a huge blood clot lodged in the mesenteric vein in Joe's small intestine. Working against time, he removed 13 decaying feet of that organ.

What had caused Jessica's clot? Her doctors at Northeast Baptist Hospital, in an effort to determine the cause, had given Jessica the requisite test for genetic factors. It had come back negative, and the probable cause of her stroke was listed as use of birth control pills—pills she'd taken for only two years. I hadn't bought this explanation because it seemed to me too coincidental that a young woman in her thirties would have a blood clot and her father, as a young man in his twenties, would also have had one.

All of this was tearing through my mind as Jessica, her face pale after her voyage through the air, lay back on her pillow with her head turned as usual to the right and tried to regain her composure.

"That was terrifying, Mom," she said. "But I'm okay now. I tell myself being up there is like being a balloonist who goes up in the sky in a basket."

"Or maybe an astronaut?" I said. As always, I had come around the bed so that we were facing one another, and I sat down sideways and held her hand.

"Did I want to be one of those when I was little?"

"You and your friend Liza both did. In first grade. We made costumes out of tinfoil."

"Funny, I don't remember that. But I remember being an octopus for a parade on Fire Island. You made the arms and legs out of old stockings."

"What about the time you were a wall for Halloween?"

"I loved being that wall. With all those pictures I drew hanging off me"

We reminisced about Halloween costumes for a while, the ones I'd made for her, the ones she'd made for Rachel and Miriam. Rachel as a storm, with a big cardboard lightening bolt across her torso and blue silk raindrops pinned to her skirt. Rachel as a butterfly, with huge cardboard wings. Miriam as a bumblebee, all yellow and black cloth coils. I didn't say a word about my tormenting thoughts about Joe. Time for them another day. But later, back in New York, I would have a very interesting conversation with a neurologist friend about clotting disorders and genetics.

"Jessica's test for genetic factors came back negative," I told him. "But the coincidence seems so clear an indication to me."

"Well, you know," my neurologist friend said. "There are thousands of genetic factors, and so far we only know how to test for a few."

I may not know in my lifetime if Jessica's stroke was the result of a genetic factor. Research into the genetic roots of common diseases such as cancer, Alzheimer's and stroke is in its infancy. This is still true, nine years after Jessica's stroke. But I remain convinced that her stroke was a genetically predetermined event. Particularly after Jessica one day reminded me of something I had long ago forgotten: Joe's parents, both of whom had suffered from thrombophlebitis—blood clots in their legs—had been first cousins.

Scientists, as well as royal families and dog breeders, have long recognized that there are congenital risks from consanguinity. When two closely related beings mate, their offspring may receive two copies of a damaged gene, one from each parent, and this can cause congenital dysfunction. I speculate that Joe's genetic inheritance may have caused his clot and that he may have passed along his damaged genes to Jessica. But I can only speculate, as so much is yet to be learned.

Writing this today, I sometimes wonder why I gave so little thought to having a child with a man whose parents were first cousins. But, of course, I was a product of my times. The 1950s, when Joe and I married, were a moment in history when old ideas about heredity were being swept aside—only to re-emerge in a new way in a matter of years.

The old ideas held that family history—nature—was of the utmost importance. Once, in connection with an article I was writing, I researched antique marriage guides, learning that very early in the 19th century, when such guides first began appearing, couples contemplating marriage were strongly advised to look for skeletons in the closets of prospective mates. Was there a grandfather who had committed suicide? A mother who'd been in a mental institution? A father who'd committed a crime and been imprisoned? The guides cautioned against having children with these mates. Such traits could be inherited, they warned. Later, this thinking solidified into the so-called science of eugenics, with proponents advocating practices such as sterilizing people with undesirable characteristics. Eugenics went out of vogue after Hitler, and so did the very idea that family history was fate. Nurture topped nature, became the new thinking. A child with a dismaying family history, if adopted, could be raised in a way that eradicated the influence of an unsavory background. Family history barely counted in the mid-1950s.

We have come full circle now. We are pressingly searching for genes that determine illnesses, both physical and psychological, and there are scientists who assert that even a tendency toward antisocial behavior can be caused by hereditary factors as much as by appalling social circumstances.

The whole matter makes me smile sometimes. It can't be often that a person sees social philosophy and scientific theory change so dramatically in her own lifetime.

It makes me smile as well to think how little, still, Joe's family's consanguinity matters to me. Perhaps had I thought more about it back when I was going to have a child, I'd not have had one. But then I wouldn't have had Jessica. How unfortunate would that have been? How much less of a joy my life?

❧

In the gym the day after my dreary conversation with Dr. Zhang, Jon saw Jessica bend her right knee. "Look at that!" her physiotherapist Beth exclaimed. For a week, Beth had been commanding Jessica, to no avail, to try to move that leg. Now, suddenly, the previously paralyzed limb had bent ever so slightly, and Jessica managed to slightly bend her left knee shortly thereafter.

Jon was so surprised when he saw that first tiny movement that he didn't quite believe his eyes. He asked Jessica to do it again, and she did. Beth called over a few other physiotherapists to witness the feat, Jon ran to get Norman to see it, Norman told some other nurses, and soon Jessica was surrounded by a crowd of awed nurses and physiotherapists.

I didn't see it happen. I was in the staff psychologist's office, complaining about Dr. Zhang.

"He's so negative," I was grousing.

"He means well," the psychologist was insisting. "He's just a bad communicator."

We were debating whether the doctor was ill-tempered or ill at ease with English when Jon burst into the office shouting, "She can move her leg! The therapists saw it! The nurses! Beth said it might mean she'll be able to walk with braces someday."

Walk. Someday. Forget about Zhang. This was Jessica, who'd kept at that bloody bike on Fire Island through bruise after bruise, through fall after fall, until at last she'd pedaled away and disappeared, headed toward the ocean, hair flying in the wind.

She'd show Zhang. I was banking on it.

⸎

Zhang's specialty was, as American medical specialties go, a relatively new one. Ever since World War I, when thousands of crippled and brain-injured soldiers returned from Europe's battlefields, doctors and nurses had been treating them with techniques employing heat, massage, and repetitive exercises. What they were doing eventually became known as physical therapy, and physical therapy began to be acclaimed not just for ameliorating the effects of battlefield injuries but for helping victims of stroke and diseases such as polio and tuberculosis. By the mid-1930s, a small group of physicians who had been studying the science behind physical therapy became convinced that physical medicine, the benefits of which were by then supported by a large body of research, was not a branch of other medical disciplines like neurology and orthopedics but a field in itself. Helped by a large grant from philanthropist Bernard Baruch, these pioneers banded together in an effort to have physical medicine recognized as a medical discipline with its own residency program, concentrated curriculum, and board examinations.

Baruch had been an intimate of Franklin Delano Roosevelt and had observed at close hand how much the physical therapy Roosevelt had received at the now famous Warm Springs Institute had aided the polio-crippled president. His gift, inspired by what had so helped his friend, enabled the physicians to begin establishing courses and research programs at universities and hospitals and continue lobbying their colleagues to recognize physical medicine as its own field. Their efforts were ultimately successful. By 1946, residencies in physical medicine and rehabilitation had been established in 25 hospitals. That same year, this new medical specialty, given the name physiatry, was officially recognized by the American Medical Association, and the American Board of Medical Specialties formally recognized physical medicine the next year.

Baruch was known for his insightfulness and way with words, and one of his famous remarks was, "There are no such things as incurable. There are only things for which man has not found a cure."

Zhang, who was skeptical about whether anything would help Jessica, decided nevertheless that if her insurance would cover the cost, he would attempt to cure her paralysis by injecting her neck and rigid left arm with the then still-experimental agent, Botox. Two days after my depressing conversation with him, the insurance company gave Zhang the go-ahead, and he gave Jessica the injections. It was no easy feat, but after several attempts, he got them into the right muscles.

Within hours, my daughter turned her head and looked at me. And it seemed likely that her occupational therapist, Will Schalla, would soon be able to start his efforts to bring her left arm down from its sash-like position across her chest. I wanted to fall on my knees and gaze upward to thank some mystical being, but, of course, it was Dr. Zhang I needed to thank—Dr. Zhang and an insurance company.

ᘐᘗ

A rehabilitation clinic's offerings for patients recovering from a stroke or from brain or spinal cord injuries consist of a great variety of treatments, not just physical exercises, although they are of central importance. Depending upon what they have been robbed of by their plundering strokes or injuries, patients may need to be helped not only to regain mobility or strength but to speak or read again, control outbursts of tears and temper tantrums or other inappropriate social behavior, take an interest in the world beyond themselves, wash themselves, use the toilet, brush their teeth or hair, put on clothes, dial a phone, get a sluggish memory to sprint a little, make poststroke dysphoria yield to at least occasional enjoyment of life. In any good inpatient rehabilitation clinic, a phalanx of occupational, recreational, and physical therapists works with specially trained nurses to maximize patients' chances of resuming the lives they once led.

The nursing care is exceedingly important. It is the nurses who must get incapacitated patients clothed and groomed and in all other ways ready to partake of therapy. Often, they are the ones who teach recovering patients how to accomplish personal tasks. Jessica couldn't do any at first, not even feed herself. At mealtimes, a nurse had to sit beside her and place bites of food in her mouth. But she was always fed in the dining room. Eating in the same room as other patients—not at bedside, as is customary with people recovering from surgery or an illness—was part of rehabilitation.

In those first days of rehab, Jessica was often dazed and exhausted. She was also in pain as parts of her body that had been inert for weeks began to have sensation—"to fire," as Will put it. He was referring to Jessica's muscles and joints. But her emotions were also beginning to fire.

More than a third of stroke patients experience poststroke depression, a singular form of the illness that many psychiatrists view as more severe than that which plagues post-heart attack victims. Poststroke depression is as much physiological as psychological. A quarter of poststroke patients have what are known as neurovegetative symptoms: a slowing down of many bodily functions, including bowel or urinary activity and the ability to swallow, speak or see; and a decided decrease in cognitive power. These losses, even when temporary, make the individual profoundly aware of having suffered a grievous injury and can bring about a shriveling of the self. Even when the losses seem minute to others, they can be overwhelming to the person affected. Eric Hodgins, a former editor at Time, Inc. who had a stroke that left him, at first, unable to read with comprehension and unable to write, wrote in an account of his recovery that it was his inability to button his shirt that plunged him into a bottomless depression: "If I could not button my shirt buttons," Hodgins wrote, "I could not appear in public; if I could not appear in public, I could no longer earn my living. And since I could not typewrite any more, regardless of where I was—interiorly some dam burst. And I found myself in a flood of tears. They were not relieving tears; they were tears of panic and despair."

Unfortunately for Hodgins, he had his stroke in 1960, before the development of antidepression or anti-anxiety medication. He was treated with lengthy psychotherapy, which was ineffective, and remained deeply depressed for many months. Today, most good rehabilitation clinics recognize the onset of poststroke depression early and quickly prescribe antidepressants.

In Jessica's case, she certainly experienced sadness as she came to realize with greater clarity what had happened to her. She didn't have many of the signs that signal deep clinical depression—the reluctance to get into activities, the inability to sleep, the loss of interest in food. But her eyes were quick to grow teary, her expression to become listless. Still, her dysphoria remained under control. Perhaps it was because of the antidepressants she was given, or because of her regular appointments with Reeves's excellent psychologist, Claire Jacobs. Or perhaps it was simply because she had an innate ability to disclaim her limitations, a particularly healthy quantity of that essential human trait, denial. It's the trait that keeps humankind going despite awareness of death and taxes, the trait that makes it possible not to see that an obstacle is insurmountable and thus, on occasion, to triumph over it. Whatever the reason, she never became so overwhelmed by sorrow that she didn't experience some degree of hopefulness—an essential factor in recovery from stroke. Without hopefulness, patients shun the strenuous demands of rehab, rejecting therapy and just giving up.

Will Schalla and several other therapists kept Jessica hopeful, promising her that if she worked with them, she could become more functional. One morning, I heard Beth say to Jessica, "It won't be easy. It'll be the hardest work you've ever done. But you've got to do it. For your girls."

Beth had met the girls, and she'd seen the parenting video Rachel's school district had produced. In the video, Jessica and Rachel had enacted a hilarious scene that featured Jessica, playing an exemplary mother, having to get Rachel, playing an obstreperous child, to do her homework. Jon had wanted the Reeves staff to see how animated and vigorous Jessica had been before her stroke, and he'd shown the little film to as many staff members as he could corral.

"I'll never be able to be a normal mother to them again," Jessica had sighed when Beth had encouraged her to work hard for her daughters' sakes.

"Sure you will," Beth had assured her. "*If* you do the work."

"I will," Jessica had promised. "For the girls."

Her longing to get well enough to raise her children made her dogged about attending her twice-daily physical therapy sessions and the group exercise class held each midday in the dining room.

She was wheeled to that class every day, from the first day she entered Reeves. On occasion, I accompanied her and watched disconsolately as at first she just sat in the back of the room in her oversized wheelchair, staring at the semicircle of patients in regular wheelchairs raising and lowering their arms. Then, one afternoon a few days after the Botox injections, I saw her begin to emulate the arm movements. Lips drawn tight from effort, she raised her right arm an inch off the armrest of her chair and continued to lift and lower it in time with the rest of the class's more energetic movements.

Hope powered those minimal but—to me—monumental achievements.

⤫

Even before Jessica managed to lift her right arm in the group exercise class, Will Schalla, with whom Jessica had quickly established a friendly, joking relationship, began his efforts to get her frozen left arm moving by doing serial casting. He started the very day after the Botox injections. "When a limb isn't actively in use," he explained to me, "the body shortens the muscles and tendons, producing contracture."

I didn't know the word.

"Tightness," Jessica interjected.

"Right," Will said. "And if the muscles are tight, the injured brain can't recruit enough of the muscle to begin active movement again."

"You talkin' about me?" Jessica sputtered, with mock indignation.

"Well you are a brain," Will said, smiling. "And you have been injured. But I wouldn't call you—"

"The injured brain? You just did."

Will laughed. "Didn't mean to." Then his brow furrowed and he began concentrating on his task, applying thin layers of plaster of Paris from Jessica's shoulder down to her wrist.

"How long will Jessica have to wear this?" I interrupted his work.

"An hour and a half, twice a day. And when it's off, we'll do some stretching. Then the next day, I'll make her a new one."

The process, he explained, was designed to put a limb into a slow, consistent stretch until contracted muscles were ready to be manually stretched and repositioned for a subsequent cast. "Think of a rubber band," Will said. "If you give a rubber band a quick stretch, it will generally snap back to its original elasticity. But if you stretch the rubber band between two doorknobs and leave it there for several days, it will assume a different length—its tightness will be eased."

Serial casting is a demanding procedure. If the stretch is tolerable and if the patient can accommodate to the pain of continual extension, serial casting can produce increased passive range of motion—which in turn opens the door to increased active range of motion. But if the stretch is too severe, it can produce unbearable pain, and the cast must be removed. Achieving the right degree of daily stretch is a tricky business.

So is the manual stretching that precedes each casting. Every day, in the hours when the cast was off, Will attempted to improve Jessica's range of motion manually—that is, to stretch her arm while she herself was passive, repetitively propelling the limb toward and away from the midline of her body.

Jessica found this part of the process excruciating. Invariably, she cried out in pain, but she trusted Will enormously. When his stretching exercises hurt her, which they always did, she looked at him in distress, her brown eyes wide and fixed on his as if asking whether all this pain was necessary. But although she flinched, she kept trying to follow his commands. And there came a day at the end of June when she felt her arm straighten a little on its own. "Oh, my God," she said, laughing and crying at the same time.

It was, Will said, "the turning point from any doubts still lingering in the back of my mind toward an unshakeable belief in her future."

❧

Ten days later, Dr. Zhang, followed by his trail of interns, asked Jessica to try to make her left hand move and was astonished to see that she could wiggle her fingers. But for the most part, despite the growing responsiveness of her arm muscles and the new mobility in the fingers, unless she was directed to do something with her left hand, she never did. She still had "left neglect," that inability to recognize—and thus try to use—her body's left side.

Disavowal of one side of the body is a common poststroke difficulty. Patients often regain good use of one side of the body but have the sensation that the other side no longer exists. It's not just that they have trouble moving the hands or limbs on that seemingly vanished side; it's that they don't even realize they have that other side.

Jessica explained this myopia of the senses to me on a day she'd received "dog therapy"—a soothing form of recreational therapy provided in many rehab clinics. With her right hand, she'd brushed the coat of a therapy dog trained to work with stroke patients, and then she'd been prompted by Dawn, the recreational therapist, to brush the dog with her left hand. "I loved grooming that dog," Jessica told me. "It had the most wonderful thick fur. But when Dawn said to use my left hand, it was really hard for me. The idea itself seemed unnatural. And the result—poor dog—was miserable. Sort of like what happens when you try to write with your nondominant hand."

To combat Jessica's left neglect, all of her recreational and occupational therapy was now being directed toward making her aware of that simple thing we all take for granted—our inherent and awesome symmetry. Learning to give herself her own pills? Her nurses made her pick them up from the table with her left hand. Playing a game of cards with Dawn? "Hold the cards in your *left* hand," Dawn insisted.

"Unfair advantage," Jessica complained. "It makes it harder for me to win."

She *could* win. Often, when she and Dawn played cards, it was Jessica who ended up with winning hands, and when they did crossword puzzles together, it was often Jessica who came up with words—the correct words—with which to fill in the white letter spaces. Moreover, sometimes the words she penciled down in ever more legible handwriting were words that she, with her background in editing, could quickly come up with but that Dawn, with her background in recreational therapy, couldn't.

And yet there were bad days. Days when Jessica couldn't bear the pain of the new casts and Will had to come, undo his work, and let her arm rest. Days when she felt like a prisoner because the muscles necessary for holding up her trunk and torso had not yet begun to fire and she still needed to be strapped upright into her oversized wheelchair, which Jon had dubbed her S.U.V.

"I'm not going to need a nurse when I go home, am I?" she asked me on one of those days, when she'd been in rehab almost a month.

"I don't know," I said, trying not to think about the possibility, always a dark shadow in the back of my mind, that her insurance company would insist she wasn't making sufficient progress and refuse to pay for more time at Reeves. I knew, and I think deep down she knew, that if that happened she couldn't go home—she'd need to go to a nursing facility. "It depends," I replied carefully, "on what you'll be able to do when you go home."

Jessica's head slumped to the side. I hadn't seen her look so unhappy in a long while. "I feel trapped," she said.

Her words made me want to weep, for it seemed to me that despite the degree of movement Will had achieved with her left arm, and despite Jessica's raising her right arm off the armrest of the chair in the exercise class, she *was* trapped. Tied into the wheelchair. I didn't know what to say, so I just nodded sympathetically.

Jon and the girls were due to arrive soon. Jon had promised the children that, on this visit, their mother would be able to play a simple game with them, the way she did with Dawn. The girls had searched eagerly through the boxes of puzzles and games that were kept in the lounge for therapy, inquired which ones Jessica might be able to participate in, and fastened on a favorite card game, Go Fish. Easy, that game. Thanks to Alice, even little Miriam knew how to play it.

When the family arrived, Jon wheeled Jessica into the lounge, and we all sat around a big table, the kids' legs pretzeled beneath their skirts, Jessica upright in her S.U.V.

But Jessica tired before the first round of Go Fish was finished and, groaning, began tugging at the strap that bound her to the chair.

"What hurts you, Mommy?" Miriam asked with an empathy

that surprised me. I'd forgotten how compassionate three-year-olds can be.

"Everything," Jessica wailed.

"Don't cry, Mommy," Rachel said.

"Don't cry, Mommy," Miriam echoed her.

The usual mother-child relationship had come undone. The children, so used to going to their mother for comfort, were suddenly having to comfort her. How, I wondered anxiously, is this going to play out? Will this role reversal stunt the children's emotional growth? Does a dire future await them? Then: Stop it, Linda! Stop thinking about the future. Just get through today. Tomorrow. The next day.

"Play again, Mommy," Miriam was begging her mother.

"I can't." Jessica was yanking at the wheelchair strap. "I feel trapped," she moaned.

"Use your imagination," Rachel, who was accustomed to using hers when she wanted to think away from something, advised. "Pretend you're not strapped down."

"You're not trapped," Miriam soothed. "You're just," she announced solemnly, "in a wheelchair."

How had the children learned to be so compassionate? Scientists believe that the tendency of human beings to respond empathetically to someone else's pain is an ancient evolutionary trait, one that chimpanzees share with us but that monkeys, less evolved, don't possess. Chimps will put an arm around a fellow chimp who's been the victim of aggression and gently pat his back. Monkeys don't do this and are even prone to shun comrades who've been attacked. Newborn human babies will cry with more anguish to the weeping of other babies than to tape recordings of their *own* crying, and by the time babies are a year old the compassion trait is in marked evidence: one-year-olds who possess the physical capability will stroke other babies who seem to be in distress or offer them a bottle or a toy. Some babies are great soothers, others less so. But the basic impulse seems common to all. And by the time babies have turned into toddlers, not just compassion but behavior that researchers deem positively altruistic is common in our species. Toddlers have been shown to come to the assistance of adults, even adult strangers, who appear to be struggling with a difficult task such as opening a jammed cabinet door or grasping an out-of-reach object. Without any prompting, encouragement, or reward, the children will spontaneously offer to help.

Still, while compassion and altruism seem to be part of our essential human makeup, emulation is also a factor in the development of these traits. A child with a nurturing parent is more likely to be empathic than a child with a harsh or abusive one. I attributed Rachel and Miriam's empathetic behavior toward their mother not just to their innate temperaments but also to Jessica and Jon's parenting, and I felt proud of them as well as of the children. At the same time, I was thoroughly dismayed by what had transpired in the lounge.

"It was so awful," I reported to Max on the phone that night. "Jessica's misery. The children trying to comfort her. All of it."

"*Vey iz mir*," Max said. "But *bubeleh*, remember, whatever you're seeing, it's for now. Just add, 'for now' to anything that bugs you."

"I'll try," I promised.

I missed him terribly. He was the most erudite man I'd ever known, with enthusiasms that ranged high and low, from Turgenev and Tolstoy to Beavis and Butt-Head, from Bach to Billie, from Larousse to latkes. He could speak Russian and Yiddish, was studying French, and talking with him over dinner was always fun. He might start with a story about haggling with the fish man behind the counter at Zabar's, our local gourmet food shop, and end with a dazzling discussion of mental health and the research he'd done into the development of psychotropic drugs. One of our friends once said that talking to Max was as thrilling as going for a ride on Coney Island's roller coaster and that his mind never slowed down for the curves.

True, all true. Yet when I'd first started going out with Max, I'd done so not for his learning and lore but because I'd sensed that he'd be a first-class stepfather. He'd made room in his heart for Jessica even when she was a cranky six-year-old who wanted her mother all to herself. She'd disdained Max in those days; he'd hidden his disappointment, wooed her with card games and the occasional muffin. After a while she dubbed him the Muffin Man, and by the time she was eight she preferred having *him* be the one to wake her in the mornings, *him* escort her to school, *him* watch Bugs Bunny with her. On Saturdays, I'd hear them laughing together at morning cartoon shows while I lay sleepily in bed.

Max and I weren't married at the time. We were spending many days and most nights together, but I'd been hesitant about marrying again. Having had a bad experience the first time around, I'd begun thinking all marriages were doomed. Still, listening to an effervescent duet of baritone and coloratura giggles on one of those weekend mornings, I decided to heave caution to the winds and marry the guy; I felt with absolute certainty that if I did, all would go well not just for me but for my first beloved, my daughter.

And it did. Things went well between me and Max's daughters, too. I'd been an extremely lucky woman—at least, I thought bitterly, until a few weeks ago. ✐

Chapter Five

Eighty Feet

THE DARK SHADOW in the back of my mind, the fear that one day Jessica's insurance company might refuse to pay for further rehabilitation, wasn't just haunting me because of free-floating anxiety, although for sure I had plenty of that. One day each week, the Reeves caseworker called Jon into her office and told him that, despite the fact that the therapists' reports indicated Jessica had made progress that week, she was not certain Jessica could be kept at Reeves any longer. "The progress may be deemed insufficient," the caseworker told Jon, regular as clockwork. "The insurance company may decline further payments." After his sessions with her, the now usually cheerful and optimistic Jon would return from the hospital in a funk. He'd retreat into long sessions at his computer, at times correcting students' papers, at other times researching baseball statistics online. The children and I would tiptoe upstairs to play a game Miriam had made up called "House Kiddie," taking turns being a Mommy and a kid. We knew without Jon saying a word that he needed to be left alone.

But Jon was, above all else, a good father. After a while, he'd emerge from his study and begin making dinner or, if I had cooked, calling the children to help him clear off the crayon-festooned dining table, assigning them kitchen tasks and making them laugh with silly jokes about the cartoon shows the three of them loved. He'd keep the household mood light until after the children were in bed, and only then fume to me about the insurance companies. "Bastards!" he exploded one evening. "They hold this sword over our heads, shove it back into its scabbard for seven days, and then out it comes again."

My feelings toward my son-in-law had undergone a dramatic change. I'd heard that stroke is frequently called the "divorce disease," that often the spouses of stroke patients can't cope with the stresses the disease ignites. They give up on their partners and even their families—fleeing, disappearing. Jon hadn't given up on Jessica or his children. He was holding his family together despite the extraordinary difficulties of doing so, even refusing my offer to pay for household help. "The kids have never been cared for by anyone but me and Jessica," he'd said. "I don't want them to have to get used to something new like that at this point in their lives." I thought him foolish but accepted his decision, which meant he took the children to day camp in the mornings, went to the hospital and visited Jessica, drove home to do his household chores and his academic work—although not teaching during the summer, he was editing a political science book—picked up the children after camp and brought *them* to the hospital to visit their mother, then took them home, made or brought in dinner, and got the girls ready for bed. It was a little easier when Alice or I was there, but neither of us could be there all the time. I never altogether forgave Jon for spiriting my daughter and grandchildren off to Texas, but I had come to respect him.

❦

"How are the kids doing?" my stepdaughter Debby asked me over the phone one evening in mid-July while I was down in Texas. Debby is a kindergarten teacher whose bountiful smile makes children immediately want to expound on their pets and plans.

"Okay, I think," I told her. But I wasn't sure. After all, Miriam was a kid who had been scared into muteness *before* her mother's illness, when Rachel had tried to get her to recite the line, "Our life is really sad now that our Mommy has died." And Rachel, what was with Rachel? Sometimes she drew pictures of robots with machine-controlled brains. I had told Jon, but he had scoffed and said, "You're reading too much into this. She sees brain-controlled robots on TV, so she draws them. Don't forget, she draws lots of pictures of girls in fancy dresses, too. Stop worrying!" But I couldn't stop. A grandmother's role is to spoil her grandchildren? Hell, no. It's to be a full-time fanatic worrier. My mind whirred with dark thoughts about the kids' emotional futures, but "Rachel's in a play," I offered to Debby. "At day camp. Miriam's beginning to read. "

"That's great," Debby said. "How old *is* she?"

"Three years and four months," I reminded her. "She read the cereal box the other day, and when she was done, she said, 'I want to read up the whole world.'"

"Oh, wow. I want to come down and see her. And Rachel," Debby said. "And Jessica."

"She'd love it," I replied. "She loves having visitors."

I used to not be sure about this, either. Not yet having regained mastery of many of her muscles, including her facial ones, Jessica often looked unresponsive. I had been troubled by this; so had various friends of hers. But I had learned that there was a discrepancy between what Jessica conveyed to others and what she was experiencing within herself. Seth Mitchell, her boss down at the county offices, had been to see her several times, both at the hospital and in rehab. They talked, she told me, about the news she watched on TV, but she had noticed that when she asked Seth questions, he didn't give her much information in reply—he just answered in brief sentences. "I must look like I'm not able to take in what he's saying," she had told me after one of his visits. "But I am. And talking with him is really motivating, like on some subconscious level it's convincing my brain that I'll be going back to work soon."

I wanted to warn Debby not to take it personally if Jessica seemed not quite with it, or if her face didn't communicate pleasure about being visited. So I cautioned her, "You may find Jessica somewhat withdrawn."

But Debby, who'd had some health issues of her own, got my drift at once. "It's okay," she said. "I get that way myself when I don't feel so hot."

"Thanks for that," I said. "Some of Jessica's friends just don't get it. They think she's not happy to see them if she doesn't smile, or doesn't engage much with them."

"Human nature," Debby replied.

Debby was right, I thought. Maybe it's only human for those of us who visit people in the early stages of stroke recovery—or, for that matter, anyone ill enough to be in the hospital—to experience some disappointment. We come out of concern and love, but it's hard to have concern and love unrequited, unacknowledged with smiles or confidences.

"I guess what's human nature is wanting to be rewarded for our caring," I said.

"Yeah," Debby agreed. "People just forget what it means to be sick, forget that a lack of responsiveness may come with the territory."

"So when do you want to come down?" I asked.

"How about this weekend?"

❧

Rachel's play was called "It's a Small World," named after the Disney parks boat ride song and written by her camp counselors. It starred all the eight-year-olds in the performing arts group. Everyone had a line or two; everyone got to sing and dance. The script told the story of some children who found a magic teleporting device. It took them from country to country, where they met up with other kids who wore their country's foreign-looking costume and spoke its foreign-sound-ing lingo. Rachel's group was transported to England, where they met kids with cockney accents and also the Queen of England. Rachel got to say "Hello," to this august personage and ask her whether she liked the Beatles. The Queen said, yes, she loved them, and all the onstage kids sang and danced to a recording of "Help!"

Miriam loved to hear Rachel rehearsing her line and bellowing out the song in their room at night. She loved it even more when Rachel deafened us with "Help me! Oooooo" while we were in the car, driving to visit Jessica. Both girls were always impatient with the ride, and when we got to Reeves, they would tear through the corridors. When we arrived at Jessica's room, though, with its growing collection of Get Well cards on the windowsills, Miriam would bound inside and make at once for Jessica's lap, but Rachel would hold back. She had been told she couldn't climb up on Jessica, that her mother couldn't support her weight. "Not yet, honey. Soon," Jessica had promised. But I wondered if Rachel believed it. She would linger at the windowsill, examining the cards, and later, while Miriam kept up a steady stream of chatter about her day, she would open the book she had brought to read, or, frowning in concentration, draw or write on one of the pads Jon kept in the room. She always said she wanted to go to the hospital and see her mother, but once she was with her, she didn't talk much to her. Perhaps it was because, being older, she was more aware than Miriam was that Jessica wasn't fully participatory. Or perhaps it was because she was, had always been, a moodier child than Miriam—one minute sunny, the next dark; one minute passionate about something she had just learned, the next sobbing in frustration over some task she had set for herself but couldn't accomplish. Whatever it was, I couldn't help thinking that what Rachel wanted more than anything in the world was a magic teleporting device that could carry her away from the sterility of hospital rooms.

❧

The best medicine for people recovering from a stroke, I read somewhere, is a daily dose of "tincture of time." Stroke is not a degenerative disease like cancer or multiple sclerosis. If a person survives the initial devastation, chances are that he or she will in time begin getting somewhat better, albeit at first by barely perceptible degrees. But time alone doesn't cure. Hard work is necessary to build muscle strength. Rehabilitation facilitates that, thus hastening and enhancing recovery, often with the most noticeable gains appearing sometime within the first three to six months.

Jessica's rehabilitation, so slow at first, had begun producing remarkable results. She had mastered a number of what Jon called her "new tricks," and every night he would tell the girls, who didn't get to see her during her gym sessions, "Mom moved her right knee all the way up to her chest." "Mom's almost strong enough to sit up by herself." "Mom's been moving her left leg a bunch."

But she had yet to stand, a necessary precursor to fulfilling her therapists' belief that, in time, she might be able to walk.

Jessica was terrified of standing. On a couple of occasions during the first weeks after the stroke, her therapists had tried to see if she could tolerate being upright. Still paralyzed, she'd been strapped onto what is called a tilt table—a flat wooden surface that can be slowly raised from a horizontal to a vertical position. Dizzy and drenched in perspiration, her eyes streaming with tears, she'd fainted both times. Several weeks later, when she'd managed to sit upright on an exercise mat for several minutes with a therapist helping her stay balanced, there'd been another attempt to get her to stand. By then fitted out with braces that went from her knees to her ankles, she'd been helped out of her wheelchair by Will and two other therapists who tried to place her against a different device, known as a standing table. This one, used for patients who did not need to be strapped in, had a chest-high armrest across the front for the patient to grasp and knee rests to support the knees.

Jessica never made it up from the chair to the standing table, despite the many hands holding her. Begging to be allowed to stay in her wheelchair, once again she passed out. But on July 16, eight weeks after her stroke, when yet again the therapists attempted to get her on her feet to lean against the standing table, Jessica stood. And she remained standing for what was considered by Will a long time—several seconds.

Tincture of time, infused with exertion and tenacity, had given her the strength, physically and emotionally, to endure, if only for those few seconds, the sublimity of full verticality. When I left Reeves that day, I was so exhilarated that, waiting in a taxi line outside the hospital, I felt for a moment that with a little effort I could have shot straight upward and flown home.

❧

"Dark!" I heard Miriam yell as I entered the house. She sped past me and we nearly collided.

"Park!" she yelled from the kitchen. Then once again, swift as a hummingbird, she ran past me, this time shouting, "Lark!" Laughing at her whirling, disappearing shape, I went from the front hall into the kitchen, and there she was again, racing through the room and calling out, "Bark! Bark!"

Debby, who'd arrived the day before, was sitting at the kitchen table. As Miriam galloped by, Debby called, "Ark!" and Miriam shouted, "Mark!" and trotted off.

"We're playing a rhyming game," Debby explained and called out to Miriam, "Trunk!"

"Junk!" Miriam shouted and was gone again.

"I was giving Miriam words," Debby said, "and Miriam was rhyming them. But she decided that was too tame and she needed a little action."

It had been all action since Debby had arrived. The kids wouldn't let go of her. If they weren't playing "House Kiddie," they were making cookies or finger-painting or donning outlandish outfits from the dress-up box. Rachel, I learned, was upstairs right then putting together costumes for a show they were going to produce for Jessica. Miriam was going to be a bride, and Rachel was going to be her flower girl as Miriam married Debby, her princely groom. I was to be in the show, too. I was to be the rabbi who wedded my three-year-old granddaughter to my 53-year-old stepdaughter.

❧

Stepchildren are a challenge. We blended families like to boast about how well we've knit the children of one family to those of another. But it isn't always easy. There's a lot of bragging, and there's a lot of denial. Many years ago, I was asked by Ed Kosner, then editor of *New York* magazine, to write a piece about merged families. Ed had two grown children with his first wife, and his second wife had just given birth to his third child. He wanted the piece to be positive and offered to help me with the research by getting me interviews with a number of his friends who, like him, had both an older set of children and a new, younger set.

"I'd like to interview some of the babies' older half-siblings," I said.

Ed didn't think there'd be any problem with my doing that. His friends had told him their older children were thrilled to have new little half-brothers and sisters to play with.

I eventually wrote the piece ("Mommy's 39, Daddy's 57—and Baby Was Just Born"), and one of the things I found most interesting about doing it was that all of Ed's friends, to a man, refused to let me interview their babies' siblings. Although they insisted to me, as they had to Ed, that their older children adored the new ones, they seemed to fear that during an interview, I might uncover some feelings they didn't want to know about.

Psychiatrists I interviewed for the article pointed out that hard-to-face feelings were quite common in merged families and warned that parents ought not to deny their existence. "When parents divorce," said one, "their children harbor the illusion that they are somehow still part of a nuclear family. But when one or the other of the parents remarries and has a new child, the last remnants of the treasured illusion are shattered. It is a very painful realization." "Never settle for denial," said another. "Keep talking about what's happened, maintain a lot of closeness, and encourage the older child to express any negative feelings he or she may have without growing defensive or angry."

Max, being a psychologist, had abided by this dictum, as had I, and although our blended family had gotten off to a rocky start— Debby, out of loyalty to her mother, had refused to come to our wedding—we had ultimately grown, over time and with full freedom to express uncomfortable feelings, to love one another unconditionally. Our family of five had expanded to include Debby's husband and their children—my other set of grandchildren—and then Jon and Jessica's children. We were a family and a team, and I was never as acutely aware of how much comfort and strength we gave each other as I was during Debby's visit.

Her presence had a beneficent effect on all of us. She got Jon talking about political missteps made by Lyndon B. Johnson. She drove me to Payless to buy new sneakers for Jessica and to Target to get her underwear. And afterward, at Reeves, while I waited in the lounge, she and Jessica had a long private talk. What did they talk about? Neither of them told me, but I figured they talked about mothering—a subject that, despite their age difference, had drawn them close—because the next afternoon, when Jon brought the children to Reeves, Jessica called out to Rachel, "C'mere, honey. I'm strong enough to hold you now."

It was what Rachel had been waiting for weeks to hear. Without a second's hesitation she flung herself across the room, climbed onto Jessica's lap, and nestled her head against her mother's chest.

"My turn!" Miriam yelled. "*My* turn!"

"No it's not!" Rachel yelled back.

"Sssh," Jessica said. "Cut it out." Then, "C'mere, Miriam, there's room for both of you." In a moment she had the two of them on her lap. And although I could see it was making her uncomfortable, she held them there, asking about their day, until Debby said, "Let's go and get a game from the lounge."

As to the wedding, which took place the following day at Reeves, Rachel wore a tutu and carried a straw basket of dried flowers, Miriam was resplendent in a long dress—one of Rachel's that came down to her toes—and Debby wore a tall paper crown she'd crafted out of shelf liner. Draped in a striped green towel that served as my prayer shawl, I asked Miriam and Debby if they'd take one another as lawful wedded partners. When they agreed, Debby presented Miriam with the gold wedding ring from her own finger and, scooping the giggling bride up into her arms, kissed her. She then gave an interview to a nurse who'd agreed to participate in our production by pretending to be a photojournalist and taking pictures of the big event. "We'll be honeymooning in Hawaii," Debby told the nurse-photojournalist. "As soon as the bride graduates from nursery school."

I hadn't observed Jessica's physical therapy for a while, so one morning after Debby left I made a point of arriving in time to see a session. When I got to the gym, Jessica was already lying on one of the mats. Beth, the therapist working with her, was trying to get Jessica to raise her hips. "Contract your buttocks," Beth directed. "Push up!"

Her face a mask of drawn lines, all her willpower directed to the effort, Jessica squeezed her dormant gluteal muscles and succeeded in raising her hips a quarter of an inch off the mat.

Beth clapped. "That was wonderful," she said. "Can you do it again?"

Once again, Jess did it.

There was more to come. When the exercise session was over, Beth lifted Jessica to a sitting position on the mat. With one hand on Jessica's shoulder and one on her back, she kept her upright. "This time I'm going to let go," Beth warned. "Can you keep yourself up?"

"No," Jess shook her head.

"Try. I won't let you fall."

A moment later Beth withdrew her hands, Jessica stayed upright for a full second before she tilted to her right side, and then to my astonishment, prevented herself from falling over by pressing her good arm down onto the mat.

"You did it!" Beth exclaimed. "You see?"

Surprised by her success, Jessica was elated. "Yes. Yes I do. And, Mom, I can do something else, too," she said as Beth transferred her from the mat to her wheelchair. "Watch."

Suddenly the chair began moving. Seated in the chair, Jessica was wheeling it herself, using both arms to maneuver it.

❦

"Do you think we've crossed a threshold?" I asked Jon that night. We were sitting in the big eat-in kitchen, Jon with his perpetual mug of tea. It was 97 degrees outside, but no matter the temperature Jon always drank hot tea, a habit that used to annoy me because it seemed so counterintuitive.

"I do," Jon said, raising his cup. "Or, at least, we're about to cross it. This evening I saw Jessica typing."

"Typing?"

"Yes. Dawn's got her doing email."

I sighed—it was a vast, oceanic sigh, welling up from deep within me—and asked Jon to pour me some tea, too.

"Guess who she got an email from?" he went on.

"Give me a hint."

"The second Mrs. Joe Wolfe."

"Ah, Bev," I said.

"She and Jim—"

"The second Mr. Bev Thierwechter," I said.

"—want to come down and visit."

"Great," I said. I loved Bev. When Joe was dying, he'd asked her to promise she'd always stay in touch with Jessica, and she had, even after she married Jim Rotherham and found herself with one more stepchild.

"Jess told me," Jon said, "that she wrote back and typed, 'Can't wait.'"

⚬

Time, which only two months ago had seemed to proceed at a funereal pace, now seemed to fly by, with every day, sometimes every hour, bringing new accomplishments, things we'd thought Jessica would never do again. In the gym, Will Schalla got her up on her feet and doing what in physiotherapy is known as proprioceptive neuromuscular facilitation. Will didn't call it that. He told Jessica they'd be doing John Travolta's stretch. "It's a stretch from D2 flexion into D2 extension," he explained to me. "But it looks like Travolta's famous 'Saturday Night Fever' dance move, where he points to the floor across his hip and then points to the ceiling. Jessica hates that exercise, but she goes along with us. It's helping her strengthen her left shoulder."

Will was a genius at figuring out ways to get Jessica doing things she hated. After much effort, he'd gotten her to take a few steps, first by holding onto parallel bars, then while supported on each side by a hand-holding therapist—and at the end of July, he decided it was time to get her to use a walker. During her physiotherapy session, he and Mariam Hammerle showed Jessica how to maneuver the wheeled device by holding it for support and then taking a step forward. Standing behind her, ready to stabilize her trunk, Will directed Mariam to crouch in front so that she could steady both the device and Jessica's left arm. But Jessica refused to take a step. "I'm scared," Jessica said. "And it hurts!" On the verge of tears, she stood stock still, imploring them to let her sit down.

"What are you afraid of?" Mariam asked.

"That I'll fall," Jessica told her. "I'll fall right onto your head."

"No, if you fall, you'll land on my lap," Mariam said soberly. Then, "And guess what? I'll ask you what you want for Christmas."

Laughing despite her tears, Jessica agreed to try. But she couldn't. Her fear of falling was so intense that it prevented her from moving.

Giving up on the attempt, Will spent the rest of the session on balancing exercises and making small talk with Jessica to get her to relax. "What's your favorite book?" he asked. "What kind of music do you like?"

The Beatles, she told him. Definitely the Beatles.

The following day, when Jessica arrived in the gym for her session with him, Will announced, "Today we're going to do Fab Four Walking," and, humming "It's Been a Hard Day's Night," he asked Jessica to sing the words.

"It's been a hard day's night," Jessica sang, "and I've been working like a do-uhg. It's been a hard day's night..."

"I should be sleeping like a lo-uhg," Will chimed in. "But when I get home to you..."

"I find the things that you do..."

"Louder," Will commanded. "Belt it out!"

With the walker parked safely in front of her, Jessica bellowed, "Will make me fee-el alright."

"You know I work all day," Mariam joined in, and while the two of them went on with the lyrics, Will directed Jessica to keep singing and try to take a step. "So why on earth should I moan," Jessica sang out, and, lifting the walker, she took a single step forward.

"Keep singing," Will said.

"Cause when I get you alone," Jessica chanted, "you know I feel okay."

"Keep moving," Will said.

And Jessica did.

That first time she managed only a few steps. But several days later, when Will announced, "Fab Four Walking again," Jessica, panting and perspiring but determined to stay on her feet, walked all the way around the therapy gym.

"Eighty feet," Will told me later. "It was an incredible step forward—and I mean the pun." ✐

CHAPTER SIX

A New Beginning

TOWARD THE END OF THE FIRST WEEK in August, a couple of Jessica's therapists hinted that it looked as if she'd soon be able to go home. She wanted fiercely to go. "I've been away from Rachel and Miriam for three *months*," she said one afternoon, then burst into tears.

"Don't cry, honey, don't cry." I spoke automatically, with that involuntary response that wells up unbidden when a mother is confronted by a child's tears.

"I can't help it," she said. "I can't stop thinking about this terrible thing that's happened to me."

It was the first time in a long while that she'd talked about what she was going through emotionally. We'd both been so eager to keep each other's spirits up that we rarely spoke of how damaged she'd been. Instead, we focused on her achievements and accomplishments.

But today we—no, she—had banged us smack up against reality. Her achievements and accomplishments were mighty. But mightier still was the fact that she'd had to make them because she'd been catastrophically wounded.

"Let's look at the bright side," I tried. "You're alive. And it looks like you're going to be able to go home soon."

"I know," she said. "I'm glad to be alive, and going home. But this terrible thing has happened, and I feel so bad."

I knew it was good that she was expressing her feelings, but I was distraught at hearing them and being unable to make things better. Facile encouragements wouldn't do. Nor would denial. What to do? I just let her talk, let her tell me things I longed not to hear because they made me feel so inadequate but which she now urgently wanted to impart.

Her voice quavering, she told me that sometimes she dreamed she was running, and that at other times, while lingering in the mist between dormancy and consciousness, she thought that her present condition was the dream and that when she awoke fully, she would be all better. Worse, she said, was coming to full consciousness, a torment that left her as miserable as when she'd first awakened from her coma and discovered what had happened to her. "It's like every single day," she sobbed, "I have to learn and accept that this is me."

I, too, was having to learn and accept this new Jessica. And I was having difficulty with the accepting part. There were times when my new, wounded daughter seemed to me like an impostor posing as the whole and perfect being I'd borne and raised to faultless young womanhood, times when I wanted to scream at the gods, "Give me back my child!" I didn't tell Jessica this. It was my dark spirit to wrestle with. So I just listened and hugged her and cried with her and said that what had happened was the worst goddamned fucking dreadful pitiful hideous thing that could ever possibly have happened. And somehow, after keening together, we both ended up feeling better.

❦

"David! Help!" I called out a few nights later to one of Jon's brothers, who was visiting us from Boston. "There's a humongous cockroach in my bathroom!" I have a preternatural hatred of cockroaches, especially the giant Texas variety, but David, long-legged and swift, bounded up the stairs and with a stomp of his size 10½ shoe demolished the creature. Afterward, Jon was angry with me: Why had I called David and not him? I'd done so, I explained, because I'd assumed he was busy on his computer, as he always was once the children went to bed. But Jon took it as an insult. And although the episode could have been funny, neither of us laughed when we found ourselves furious with each other over one dead bug.

Nor was it funny when we had a big dust-up over a computer desk I bought at an outlet store. I'd purchased it because, encouraged by Jessica's progress, I'd started working on that last chapter of my *Chapman* book, and there was no space other than the cluttered dining room table for me to set up my laptop and spread out my research. Jon was annoyed that I'd added furniture to his and Jessica's house without permission.

"This is not your house," he reminded me sharply.

"Don't worry, I'm planning on shipping it home when I leave," I sputtered. To me, his objection to my getting the desk seemed a clear instance of male chauvinism—he had a desk at which to work, but he didn't credit that I too had work and needed a place to do it.

To Jon, however, my buying the desk was a major transgression of the rules of in-law living. "No," he steamed, "I'm just saying. I just think you should have asked me."

Later, that little desk would become one of the household's most cherished items. But at this point in Jessica's recovery, both Jon and I were on edge about her imminent return home, and apprehension was making us prickly all over again. He was worried about making the house Jessica-safe. Would he need to install an elevator? A ramp alongside the front doorstep? What would that cost? And what about getting stair railings and bathroom safety bars? I was worrying because once Jessica was home and no longer in the care of doctors, nurses, and therapists, Jon would be in charge of looking after her—and I didn't trust him to keep her safe. I was still filled with self-recrimination for returning to New York that day after Mother's Day, thereby failing at a mother's prime duty: protecting her child from harm. I would always be angry with myself for this, however irrational the anger was. But I was even angrier at Jon, still obsessing over why *he* hadn't protected Jessica, why he hadn't noticed how sick she was that day and gotten her to a hospital before she became incoherent. Suppose, now that she was coming home and he was in charge of her, something went wrong. Would he once again fail to get help swiftly?

My notes from those days are embarrassing. I was incorrigibly cranky and upset by things Jon said, or didn't say, and by things he did, or didn't do. But as George Orwell once said, a memoir that does not tell something disgraceful about the author cannot be trusted.

Tuesday, August 6
Bev and Jim were visiting Jessica today when Bev learned that Jessica's Coumadin isn't thinning her blood sufficiently. I panicked when she told me this, but when I discussed it with Jon he told me it'll be all right. They'll soon get it adjusted....

Jon doesn't worry. For him, like Candide, everything is, if not all for the best, like Candide, all always about to be for the best.

Wednesday, August 7
Jon says the Coumadin dose has been straightened out. But of course Jessica will have to take Coumadin for the rest of her life, and that alone worries me. It's a dangerous drug. Too little and she runs the risk of developing another blood clot. Too much and she could bleed internally. And die.

Bev told me not to fret so much about the Coumadin.

"Joe took it all his life," she reminded me.

"Yeah," I said. And ignoring the fact that Joe had died of a cause unrelated to Coumadin, shot back at her, "But he didn't live so very long, did he?"

Saturday, August 9
Bev thinks Jess is going to need a home health worker if and when she goes home. I do, too. But Jon doesn't envision her needing a whole lot of care. So he doesn't want a helper, insists he can handle it all. The kids. And Jessica.

He's not objecting because of the cost. Max and I have told him repeatedly we'd pay. It's his provinciality. His family never had household help so he thinks it's somehow unseemly. "I don't want a stranger in the house," is his explanation.

It drives me up the wall. Because I'm sure that the fewer household chores he has when Jess gets home, the better the attention he can give her. But he won't budge on the matter. It's like, "This is the way I wanna have it, and that's that."

End result was: I kept nagging Jon about bringing in help in classic hypercritical mother-in-law fashion. And he kept stubbornly ignoring what I said in classic resistant son-in-law fashion. To top matters off, when I told him about the conversation I'd had with Bev about Joe's having been on Coumadin all his (short) life, Jon said—quite as if he'd not have thought of telling me this if I hadn't brought up Coumadin—that the medication still wasn't thinning Jessica's blood sufficiently and she was getting injections of Lovenox to boost its effects.

"Why didn't you tell me?" I snapped. And Jon, my Candide-son-in-law, just pooh-poohed my concern and said, "They're working on it. They'll get it under control."

Jessica's Coumadin dosage *was* eventually brought under better control. And Jon and I eventually made up, as we invariably did. A couple of days after my outburst, I wrote in my journal:

> *I apologized to Jon for having been so crabby with him. He said, "It's okay. I've forgotten about it."*
>
> *"Oh, too bad." I joked. "If you've forgotten about it, why did I bother apologizing?"*
>
> *He was quick on the draw. "I mean," he said, "now that you've said you're sorry, I've forgotten about it."*
>
> *"Nice touch," I snorted. He laughed, and then I did, too, and the turbulent air between us cleared.*

These spats might have gone on forever if it weren't for Jessica's now constant signs of improvement. The following week she walked all around the gym by holding onto Will and Mariam's hands. She went "swimming" in a hospital pool: Mariam pushed her special waterproof wheelchair down the pool's ramp and, aided by weightlessness, she was able, with the therapist's help, to get up from the chair and walk nimbly in the water. She did her laundry in Reeves's laundry room, and she began regaining culinary skill in a kitchen used for cooking instruction. One day, she baked brownies, measuring the ingredients precisely with no help from the supervising occupational therapist. Another day, she made her famed chicken with honey and soy sauce, a recipe she'd inherited from my mother. Still another day, she prepared a salad that boasted Max's signature lemon vinaigrette, albeit after being chided by Dawn and Kathy for not handling her knife in a safer manner when she sliced her cucumbers.

"You won't be cutting food when you go home, will you?" I asked when she reported this kitchen episode to me. My overprotective instincts were in full gear.

"Well, I certainly intend to do some of the cooking," she replied. "*Sooo*, Mom," she went on, giving me the exasperated look I remembered having received many times when she was a teenager, "If I'm cooking, sometimes I'll have to be cutting. *Right*, Mom?"

"Yeah," I allowed. "Yeah, I guess so."

In addition to familiarizing herself once again with chores like washing clothes and cooking, Jessica was also now doing email regularly, and soon she was in touch with a host of friends and cousins. Her college roommate, Marcy. Her best friends from high school. Her cousin Jef in North Carolina. Her cousin Greg in Japan. She and Greg were exactly the same age. His mother and I had laid our babies side by side on a blanket when they couldn't yet crawl and giggled as they aimlessly batted at a big colored ball. They'd held hands and taken some of their first steps together. They'd wailed for Bambi and quailed for E.T. And, as in a French film, as so many age-matched cousins do, they had exchanged their very first exploratory kiss.

Jessica's accumulating skills convinced the staff at Reeves that she was indeed nearly ready to go home. And at the end of August, 13 weeks after the stroke that had catapulted my daughter so close to death, Jon was informed that he and Jessica could spend a night together in the room that had so enchanted me when we first visited Reeves: the "real world" room. Just as I had fantasized, they'd be watching TV from the puffy couch, sharing sleeping quarters, and fixing a breakfast of toast and eggs in the little kitchenette. In the morning, if all proceeded as well as expected, Jon would be taking Jessica home. Reeves had made this miracle possible.

"God, we were fortunate in having her at Reeves," I said to Jon when he told me the news.

"You bet," he cheered.

But how fortunate we had been became clearer than ever a while later, when Dr. Zhang examined Jessica for the last time. By then, she'd become quite fond of him. "He isn't always negative," she'd told me. "In fact, sometimes he's positively encouraging." He could be humble, too, I discovered after that last examination. "He told me," Jessica reported, "that when I applied for admission to Reeves, he didn't want to take me because, judging from my CT scans and MRI, he didn't think Reeves would be able to help me.

He told me, 'I only agreed to take you as a favor to a colleague.'"

Humility in doctors is a rare trait. So few of them are willing to admit to having made a mistake or being wrong. That Zhang had done so impressed me no end. He didn't name the colleague who'd asked him for this favor, and I didn't inquire, but I felt pretty sure I knew who it was. And after Jessica informed me of that conversation, any reservations I'd had about having tried to pull strings to get her into Reeves vanished. Were anyone to ask me now if she should use personal connections to get herself or one of her children the very best and fastest medical care, I'd scoff and say, "Are you kidding?"

⚭

The house on Oak Sprawl was ready. To the surprise of her therapists, Jessica had climbed a full flight of stairs at Reeves, and she'd decided she wouldn't need an elevator to go upstairs at home, just an additional banister on the staircase to the bedroom, and Jon had gotten a carpenter to do the work. I was over my fits of anxiety. Jessica was doing so well that my fears about her ability to manage at home had begun evaporating. As to the girls, they were ecstatic at the good news. When Jon told them Jessica would soon be home, Miriam pranced around the house chanting, "Mommy's coming, Mommy's coming," and that afternoon, after preschool, enlisted Rachel's help in stringing up a huge Welcome Home sign that she and her classmates had made in school that day. In the evening, when I was attempting to unsnarl the nest of tangles that gathered anew in her long auburn hair every day, a squirming Rachel announced, "I can't wait till Mommy's here!" And then, "She's better at this than you."

Pretending to be insulted, I pouted, and Rachel patted my head. "Who got your tangles out when Grandma Alice or I wasn't here?" I asked. "Did Daddy do it for you?"

"No, he's worse at it than you are," Rachel said. "I did it myself. I did Miriam's, too."

I told her she was wonderful and that doing Miriam's hair had been really good of her.

I was surprised by her reply. "All the teachers at school kept saying how wonderful I was while Mommy was sick. I didn't like it."

"Why not?" I asked, trying to brush with a little less force.

"I didn't want," she announced theatrically, "to be thought of as someone who was in the middle of a tragic situation."

"But you sort of were," I interposed.

"I hated it. I didn't want to be the only person in second grade without a mother," Rachel said. "Divorced mothers don't count."

⸎

Although Jessica and Jon knew they were going to need some help from Alice and me once Jessica was established at home, they had requested privacy on the first few days—no mothers or mothers-in-law anywhere in the vicinity of San Antonio. They wanted to explore this new, perhaps smooth, perhaps rocky promontory of life on their own. So I was back in New York on Friday, August 30th, when an impatient Jon, with two excited little girls in tow, pushed Jessica through the swinging doors of Reeves, into an elevator, out along the maze of corridors that led to the exit of University Hospital, and into a dazzling late-summer afternoon. I heard all the details over the phone that evening from an exhausted but exultant Jessica. I heard how Rachel and Miriam had bounded into Reeves exclaiming to all they encountered, "We got out of school early so we could bring Mommy home!" I heard how several therapists had gotten teary-eyed and told Jessica to be sure to visit them when she came back to the center for outpatient therapy, how Mariam had said she'd been doing this work for nine years and had never seen a patient make the miraculous recovery Jessica had made, and how Miriam had climbed up onto Jessica's lap in the wheelchair and whispered in her ear, "I have a secret to tell you, Mommy. It's special to be home."

I heard all that, and, a while later, Rachel showed me a little school essay she wrote in third grade about the event:

Miriam and I slept over at a friend's house the night before we took Mommy home. I was acting sullen and sad, the way I'd been acting at school. But suddenly I realized my mom must have had it much harder than I did, and I brightened up. I was ready! In the morning I left school early and we went to the hospital. And as I stepped with my mom into the sixth floor elevator, it was like I was stepping away from all my problems.

Some people outside the family have trouble believing Rachel wrote this essay in third grade, but she has always been something of a prodigy.

I felt pretty much the way Rachel did when Jessica first came home. Problems gone. Vanquished. I felt the way I feel every New Year's Eve, knowing on a rational level that, just like the years before it, the one about to arrive will have its low points, rough patches, disappointments, but on some other, mindless level, believing with mystical faith that this one would be different, would be a sublimely *happy* new year. I felt the way I always feel when I spot the first spangle of golden daffodils in Central Park. When I feel the first warm breezes waft through my open windows. When I shove my down coat to the back of my closet, knowing that spring has definitely arrived and greeting its appearance with inexplicable optimism. My mother used to tell me that my grandfather, a Russian immigrant who lived behind his basement tailoring shop in Brooklyn, would insist, every spring, on being driven outside the city to see the pale green leaves on the trees along the highway. "Before they're full green," he would say. "I want to see the new beginning."

Jessica's return home was New Year's and spring, a new beginning for me. For Max, too. A good dancer, in the early years of our marriage he used to whirl me around in the kitchen while we cleared up after dinner. For a long time lately, his back had been aching too much for dancing, but after that first call Jessica made to us from home, he pulled me up from my chair and, humming "As Time Goes By," put his arm tight around me and began executing a rhythmic foxtrot.

∽

Jessica had come home from Reeves in a wheelchair. She'd elected to sleep in the familiar upstairs bedroom she and Jon had always shared rather than have a cot set up for her in the living room. But the staircase to the bedroom had 14 steps. Starting with her first night at home, Jessica made her way up at night using the grueling stair-climbing technique she'd been taught at Reeves—placing her arms on two banisters and heaving herself upward to the next step with a mighty pull.

I saw her execute this demanding climb when I came back to Texas shortly after her return home. Each night, when Jessica felt ready to begin the ascent to the bedroom, she would get out of her wheelchair and, holding onto the banisters for support, stand at the bottom of the stairs while Jon carried the chair to the top. Then he'd hurry down and position himself at the bottom of the staircase, hoping that if Jessica tumbled backward he'd be able to break her fall. Sometimes she'd teeter between steps and I'd gasp. But she'd find her balance and keep climbing. I'd watch and wonder. Was she mine? How had I ever managed to produce this resolute person? I had plenty of time to contemplate these questions as she struggled slowly upward toward the top of her own private Everest. When she reached it and sat down in the safety and comfort of the wheelchair, my sigh of relief was in time with her audible sigh of triumph.

I stood nervously at the bottom of those stairs day after day as Jessica made her ascent, until I finally realized there was little chance of her tumbling down. Beth's exercises had made her legs strong, Will's had strengthened her arms, and she was clearly able to perform her climbing feat without endangering herself.

I went back and forth between New York and Texas often the first weeks she was home. Marcy, Jessica's college roommate, had taken up a collection among several friends in their circle to provide Jessica and Jon with a bimonthly cleaning service. But bimonthly cleaning went just so far in a house with two young children. One of my jobs when I was in San Antonio was to sweep and mop and deal with the always accumulating clutter of toys, books, and clothes. Another was to accompany Jessica to her outpatient physical therapy sessions and to a lab to get her blood drawn. Coumadin, the blood thinner she was on, must be carefully titrated, and because her Coumadin levels were still erratic, we had to visit the lab regularly.

It also occurred to me that I'd best apply myself to getting my ravaged daughter looking less haggard. She was thin as a shadow and needed clothes that didn't hang on her like sacks. Her hair wanted cutting; her eyebrows needed shaping; her fingernails were cracked; her hands chapped. School had started up again, not just for the girls but for Jon as well. In the mornings, he would drop the children off at school and then proceed to the university, and on days when Jessica didn't have a lab visit or a therapy session scheduled, we'd go clothes shopping or to the local beauty salon— mother-daughter expeditions we hadn't made together since she was a teenager.

Her therapy was devoted now primarily to getting her out of the wheelchair and able to manage ever-increasing distances with a walker. After practicing its use for several days in therapy, she was instructed to use the walker as often as she could when she was in her house. She was also given finger exercises to improve her dexterity, arm exercises to improve her arm strength, and creative writing assignments to prepare her to go back to work as a researcher, writer, and editor. Indeed, no deficit was deemed too small not to be harpooned with a thrust of highly specific exercises.

In the afternoons, we'd come home. "I'm *so* tired, Mom," Jes-

sica invariably said, her head beginning to nod as soon as she finished the last bite of an afternoon snack. I wasn't surprised. Poststroke patients need a great deal of rest. For most, it takes months
to regain the ability to get through a whole day without napping.
Curling up in the new cushioned recliner Bev and Jim had bought
her, Jessica would sleep for several hours while I did chores and
helped Jon prepare dinner. Miriam never wanted a real dinner.
"I just want a dinner snack," she'd say, which, translated, always
meant a peanut butter and jelly sandwich.

By the time dinner was over, Jessica was exhausted again. "Dog-
tired," she'd say, which always made the children laugh and cavort
around on all fours until they fell down in a giggling heap under
the table. But Jon, eager to have Jessica resume some of the domestic tasks she'd previously taken care of, would pile a heap of newly
washed clothes alongside where she sat, and no matter how tired
she was, Jessica would fold and sort and stack. Or she'd get on the
phone to arrange play dates and after-school pickups for the girls.

I'd get busy readying them for bed. Miriam required a game
or two after her bath. She'd outgrown "House Kiddie," so mostly
now we played "Doctor." Rachel and I took turns being doctor or
nurse, and Miriam brought a pile of dolls to see us professionals for
help with their various ailments. Of one, we were informed, "Her
nose is sick." Of another, "She has the flu." Of a third, "Her legs
got bended." Of a fourth, she said one night, "Her head is broken."

That complaint sounded scary. "How did that happen?" I
asked Miriam.

"She was having a dream," Miriam said. "And there were bad
people in it. And they broke her head."

"Dreams, you know, aren't real," I said, not sure if she knew
this or not.

"I know," she announced. "But this was a *real* dream."

Like mine, I thought. Poor Miriam, dreaming her baby doll
had a broken head. Poor Miriam. She'd had a variant of my now
almost vanquished nightmare.

◦⊱⊰◦

Max hadn't been able to get away from work since Jessica had come home. But early in October, he took time off to join me in Texas for a long weekend. When Jessica and I saw Max's cab from the airport coming up her driveway, I said, "I'll go," and headed for the front door.

"No, me," Jessica said. Rapidly, she maneuvered the walker to the front door, opened it with a free arm just as Max rang the doorbell, and, leaning forward awkwardly over the walker, flung an arm around him.

"Oh, pussycat!" Max exclaimed. "Oh, *bubeleh*, you're walking! The last time I saw you, you were *oyf kapores*."

"Whatever that means," Jessica groaned, then laughed. She rarely understood his Yiddish expressions, but in the way that puns do, those expressions generally produced exasperation mingled with amusement. "So what am I now?" she asked. "With kapores? Out of kapores?"

"Never mind," Max said. "Now you're just beautiful. A sight for sore eyes. My best, most beautiful *bubeleh*."

I got Max a drink, and he settled down alongside Jessica in the living room and began quizzing her about her recent activities. Max had a keen interest in other people and a way of listening and hearing not just what they said but what they didn't say, the things that lay beneath their verbal communication. I could never decide if this interest and ability was the result of his professional training or if he'd gone into psychology because he already had the interest and ability. What I knew was that I envied his way of getting others to open up to him, and that I wished I, too, had this unique talent. Now, as he and Jessica talked, I heard her tell him things about her hospital stay that, out of her inclination to always sound positive around me, she had kept hidden. The bad things. The sad things. The daily humiliation of having nurses oversee her bladder and bowel functions. The tension at having to wait when nature called until an aide arrived to help her onto a commode. The anger at passive-aggressive nurses, like the one who'd said to another within Jessica's hearing, as if like a cat or dog she couldn't comprehend human speech, "This one's never going to recover. Her husband should sign a DNR order." And the one who had cruelly berated her for impatience and other poststroke behavioral tics she had not yet learned to control.

Sensing that my presence might be an obstacle to their communication, I left the room and went out into the backyard, where, swiveling around on the children's swing, I thought once again how fortunate I'd been in my choice of a second husband and a stepfather for my daughter. When Max and I were dating, I used to obsess about the fact that, shortly before meeting me, he'd left his first wife after 25 years of marriage, and fret over whether, given this, I could trust him with my love. "I mean, a man who'd leave a wife after all that time," I'd worried to my closest friend. Ann had said, "Well, if you get twenty-five years out of this marriage, you'll be plenty lucky." Now, that very month, we had been together 32 years.

⚬⚬⚬

With Max around, life was always festive, and so it was that weekend. True to his reputation as a bon vivant, he had decided we should stay in a hotel rather than at Jessica and Jon's house so we'd be able to entertain the family, treat them to meals none of us would have to prepare in a hotel's well-appointed café, and let the children swim in a hotel's spacious pool. He had chosen a particularly attractive place with park-like grounds, where the children were able to roam through a mini-forest of Texas oaks playing "Running Away from Home" and Rachel's new favorite, "Explorer." Max also insisted that we adults leave the girls with a neighbor on Saturday night and dine downtown with Marvin and Ellie, who were friends of the chef at a fabled San Antonio restaurant.

Jessica, who hadn't been out at night since that long-ago dinner at the Chinese restaurant with its now so ironic-seeming Good Luck banners, put on makeup and set aside her usual uniform of jeans, dressing up for the occasion in a flouncy skirt. She went in her wheel-chair—she'd been told by her therapists to use the walker just in the house at present—and looked fatigued from her preparations as Jon pushed her to our table. But she quickly revived when Max ordered a bottle of Taittinger and we lifted our glasses to toast her recovery.

Marvin wanted to hear about her outpatient therapy. She told him about learning to use the walker, and about the finger exercises she was doing to increase her fine motor coordination, as well as about a new program designed to retrain patients to do whatever work they used to do. "It's called Advanced Cognitive Therapy," Jessica explained.

"Sounds," Ellie observed, "like a college course."

"In a way it is," Jessica said wryly, "because you have to get accepted to take it. And there's a prerequisite—which is a stroke."

The chef sent us rounds of starters—dainty quail eggs, lime-drenched sea urchins, velvety foie gras—and between bites and murmurs of pleasure, Marvin asked, "What are you doing in the program?"

"My first assignment is to summarize a medical journal article my therapist gave me about behavioral problems in the brain-injured," Jessica said, chewing as heartily as the rest of us. "I've been working on it"—she nodded at Max as she spoke—"and I'm going to append a note saying the article should be required reading for all rehab nurses. Because some of them just don't get that many of their patients' behavioral problems are caused by temporary cognitive deficits."

I'd known about the assignment, but not about the note. How splendid, I thought while admiring an onion tart small enough for Tom Thumb. She's gone from talking about being humiliated by insensitive nurses to directing her anger toward helping others who might find themselves in the same boat. Had Max had a hand in this? I couldn't be sure, but Max *was* something of a wizard.

His wizardry—or perhaps it was just chance—brought my friend Dean back into our lives on the day of Max's departure for the airport. Jessica, Jon and the girls had come to the hotel for a farewell brunch, and we were all carrying bits and pieces of Max's luggage and waving at the taxi line outside the hotel when a cab pulled forward and the driver leaped out. It was Dean. I was so stunned that I dropped two of the three books I was carrying that Max was hoping to read on the plane. Dean picked them up, and then there were hellos and introductions and even hugs as I introduced him to my daughter for the first time. "Didn't I tell you?" he trumpeted to me. And to Jessica, "I *told* your mother you'd be up on your legs."

Two days later, a small Styrofoam box appeared on Jessica and Jon's front door stoop. Inside were two plastic containers: one of stewed lamb and the other of rice mixed with nuts and raisins and slivers of dried apricots.

The food was delicious and we ate it all.

❧

I knew that while Jessica was happy to be home, being there was something of a mixed blessing. Returning home is never easy for anyone who has had a long hospital stay. For poststroke patients, it inevitably produces a tangle of contradictory emotions: joy at being back in familiar surroundings mixed with the unnerving realization that things are not the same for them in those familiar surroundings, and may never be. Back when I'd been trying to learn as much about stroke as I could, I'd read the autobiography of the actress Patricia Neal, who, like Jessica, had suffered a stroke in her late thirties. Still impaired when she was released from the hospital, Neal wrote about her homecoming, "Every minute brings new reminders of the terrible gaps between you and every single thing you have taken for granted all your life. Brushing your teeth, swatting a fly from your face, getting a drink of water, going to the bathroom in the middle of the night."

For Neal, the disconnect between what she had been capable of before her stroke and what she was capable of when she first got home from the hospital produced fury, a fierce anger that grew with each reminder of what she had lost. For editor and writer Robert McCrum, whose memoir about his stroke I'd also turned to for information, the return home, exhilarating at first, was soon followed by depression. Obsessed with his disabilities and beset with frustration, he wrote, depression "rose up and engulfed [me] like a wave.... In my depression I was drugged by sleep, drugged and oppressed and anesthetized and stupefied by its powers. I spent hours and hours asleep. I could sleep late into the morning. Or I could sleep before lunch, and in the early afternoon. I could sleep as the day faded, and again before nightfall. I could sleep early or late, regardless of whether I had spent even twenty of the previous day's twenty-four hours unconscious. The sleep monster had me in his jaws, and I was happy to be under the covers with him."

Jessica, too, had her bouts of anger and depression upon realizing her limitations, but most of the time she managed to keep her spirits up. In part, it was the presence of the children that made this possible. There was no way, with two demanding youngsters, that she could retreat into endless hours of sleep. Moreover, she was unwilling to have her daughters view her as a handicap to them emotionally as well as physically, and, as a consequence, kept her blue moods to herself.

In part, too, she was buoyed by the physical therapy she was still receiving on a daily basis as an outpatient at Reeves. There, cheered on by a different group of optimistic therapists, she kept pushing herself to become ever more mobile.

But achieving that desired mobility, it soon became clear, was going to be exceedingly difficult. Dismayingly, one part of Jessica's brain had been so damaged that it had yet to show signs of developing new neural pathways to replace certain dead nerves: specifically, those that controlled her ability to flex her feet, wiggle her toes and sense exactly where she was placing her feet—all important to being able to balance without the help of braces. The stroke had left her with some sensation in her feet and ankles and the ability to point her feet, but that was all.

Jessica's doctors hoped that with repetitive patterning exercises of the kind that had developed the necessary pathways elsewhere in her body, this unresponsive part of her brain might also be revived. However, to be able to do the patterning exercises, she needed to wear her braces. And even with the braces, walking required as much mental as physical exertion. Jessica had to control the placement of each step she took by first, in effect, "telling" her feet where to go.

She threw herself into the training, and eventually her efforts began to pay off. Five months after her stroke, she was staying out of the wheelchair and using her walker for two-hour stretches at a time. Seven months after her stroke, she went from using the walker to using a four-pronged cane. Nine months after her stroke, she graduated to a regular cane. And 17 months after the stroke, my granddaughters sent me a kind of diploma, a handwritten document that looked like this:

On this day of Oct 9, 2003 the woman

Jessica Bernstein

has walked without a cane!

Rachel Bernstein
Daughter

_____ M
Daughter

From that time forward, Jessica only needed to use a cane when she went out of the house. ✎

CHAPTER SEVEN

I'm Her Mother

WITH JESSICA'S RECOVERY proceeding so well, I stopped going down to Texas as often as before. But my daughter and I stayed in close touch via phone and email, and she continued to surprise me with impressive accomplishments. One was learning to drive again. Although she hadn't had to relinquish her driver's license after the stroke, her occupational therapist had encouraged her to take and pass a driving evaluation to ensure she could still drive safely. Eager, she'd taken some brush-up lessons until she felt adept. But when she went for the evaluation early in the winter of 2003, she failed it. Returning home in a funk, she told Jon dismally, "Zhang said I'd never be able to drive. He said I wouldn't have the muscle memory for it."

"He said a number of things that turned out to be wrong," Jon reminded her and told her she'd just have to try again.

Jon could be tough like that. Had I been there, I'd probably have said, "Oh, poor baby," and tried to commiserate her misery away. I'd probably have done that all those times she said she was dog-tired and Jon put a pile of laundry in front of her. Or when he called to say he'd be home late and she should start the girls' dinner by herself. But I was beginning to recognize that if I'd been in charge of Jessica's rehabilitation, she might never have made the strides she'd made. She and Jon had a partnership, one in which there was work to be done by both. I had a different relationship with Jessica. Because she'd been my baby once, I was still inclined to baby her, not make demands on her. That wasn't, I was coming to realize, what she needed, or even wanted. At Jon's insistence, she went back in the spring for more driving lessons. In June, she passed the driving evaluation with exemplary ease.

Becoming a driver again made a universe of difference both for Jessica and for the family, enabling her to relieve Jon of some of the many duties he'd had to perform on his own ever since her stroke. Now, she started sharing with him the curse of suburban living, the incessant chauffeuring of children: driving the girls to school, picking them up afterward to deliver them to after-school activities, taking them shopping for the constantly necessary bigger shoes and next-size pants and tops. It helped that she had a handicap permit. She'd park close to whichever supersized Texas store they'd chosen as their destination. Then, with the children racing in front of her, she'd make her way inside with her cane and snag a motorized scooter with which to navigate the store's vast distances.

She was still challenging herself to do more, and do better.

There was the day in early summer—I was in San Antonio on this momentous occasion—when the girls kept clamoring all morning to be taken swimming at the neighborhood pool and none of us wanted to oblige them. Jon hated swimming, I had a cold, and Jessica couldn't go into the pool because it didn't have a railing alongside the steps leading down to the water. She couldn't wear her braces into the water, and without them it was impossible for her to manage steps that lacked a handrail. Yet after lunch that day, she said to me, "Come on. Let's go. I think I've figured out how to get into the water."

"How?" I asked.

"You'll see," was all she would say.

She drove us to the pool. The kids, already in their bathing suits, bounded shoeless out of the car as soon as she turned off the ignition, burning the soles of their feet on the parking lot's tarmac and hot-footing it toward the pool. There were lifeguards at the pool, so Jessica waved to let the girls know it was okay for them to go into the shallow end. Then she spread a towel on the stone siding at the deep end, sat down on it, removed her braces and, thrusting her legs in front of her, slowly inched her body forward until she was right at the pool's edge, where, leaning heavily on her arms, she lowered herself into the deep part of the water. A moment later she was swimming toward the shallow end. "Yay, Mommy!" I heard Miriam shout. And then Rachel: "Hurry up, Mom, and come play!"

There was the day at the autumn school fair—I wasn't there but was told about it—when Rachel, who sometimes seemed convinced her mother could still do everything she used to do, wanted Jessica to wiggle hula hoops with her. Jessica told Rachel that wouldn't work but, not wanting to disappoint her altogether, agreed to play musical chairs, moving as fast as she could along the rows of seats, her cane in one hand, her other hand grabbing at chair tops to steady herself. At Thanksgiving time, she flew to New York with Jon and the girls and went to see the ice skaters at Rockefeller Center, managing to stay on her feet for several blocks until she found a ledge to sit down on and rest. And by December she felt ready to do something she hadn't expected she'd ever be able to do again: go to Disneyland. Jon's parents had frequently taken him and his siblings there when they were children, and Jon had such happy memories of the amusement park that he'd wanted Jessica to see it. He'd taken her there right after they were married, and the two of them had taken Rachel as soon as she could toddle. It troubled Jessica that, because of her disability, Miriam was being deprived of the Disney experience. So, despite some worries about whether she could handle the crowds, she'd decided to attempt the trip, and at Christmas time the family went to Anaheim.

I have pictures of that trip. Because of the great distances they were to traverse, Jon is pushing Jessica in a wheelchair. The children are giggling and making faces for the camera, held by some cooperative passerby, and Jessica is wearing a broad smile of satisfaction.

When I told a California cousin of mine that they were visiting her state, she told me a story about the great violinist Itzhak Perlman, crippled by childhood polio, who walks with crutches and braces. According to my cousin, one night at Lincoln Center, Perlman broke a string right in the middle of a symphonic concert. The conductor laid down his baton, but rather than wait for someone to bring him a new string, Perlman signaled the conductor to start the music again and continued playing with only three strings. When the concert ended to a round of thunderous applause, Perlman bowed and said to the audience, "Sometimes you have to find out how much music you can still make with what you have left."

Most likely apocryphal—Perlman never acknowledged having made that statement—this story nevertheless found its way into print, garnering numerous testimonials from people who claimed to have been present at the concert and heard Perlman's words. True or not, I thought Jessica would enjoy the story, so I recounted it to her.

She was, indeed, delighted by it. "That's it," she remarked. "That's *my* philosophy."

Alas, it wasn't mine. As the months after Jessica's stroke accumulated, life for all of us became normal, okay, even good. Miriam entered kindergarten. Rachel won a citywide poetry contest. *The Murder of Dr. Chapman* came out. Jessica started working again, taking on freelance editorial jobs. Jon, having failed to produce the conventional number of academic articles due to the time he'd had to devote to Jessica's recovery, was denied tenure at his university, but he began writing a political blog that quickly became widely read and turned him into an often-quoted pundit. Max retired and went regularly to the opera and ballet. But Jessica still had to wear braces when she walked, and I was having trouble resigning myself to that fact.

I still lingered a lot of the time in some dreamland where none of what had happened to my daughter had ever occurred. I was like a friend of mine, a woman more prone to prayer than I, who said to me after her preschool-age granddaughter was stricken with encephalitis, "It's so bizarre. First you long just to have the kid survive. You tell God you'll do anything, *anything*, if only He'll let her live. And then, when He does, but she doesn't walk or talk properly, you begin bargaining: 'Please, God, I'll do anything, *anything*, if you'll just make her disabilities go away.' And when He does, but you still see little imperfections, things that others don't seem to notice but that worry the life out of you, you're mad at God: 'Why couldn't You make her completely perfect, the way she used to be?'"

I, too, wanted perfection. I still wanted Jessica exactly the way she used to be. No matter that I had her alive, and with all her personality and mental faculties intact. I couldn't accept that although she was now able to walk with the assistance of her braces, she couldn't walk without them. Nor, as we eventually learned, was she likely ever to be able to do so. The nerves in the area of her brain that controlled sensation and motor control in her ankles and feet had been damaged beyond repair, and no new neural pathways had developed to take on their work. With the help of therapy, she had regained some ability to wiggle the toes on her left foot—and would later regain some ability to flex her right foot—but after a year and a half of outpatient physical therapy, Jessica was told there was nothing further that physiotherapy could do for her.

"Nothing?" I asked, dismayed.

"Nothing," Jessica told me. "But I've joined a gym. My physical therapist said that using a treadmill will at least let me keep strengthening my ankles."

❦

One day, about six months later, Jessica emailed me that her North Carolina cousin, Jef—Joe's sister's son—had written to her that he'd been delving into family history and had discovered that, according to family lore, their grandparents, Lily and Jack Wolfe, were related to the Marx Brothers. He'd also learned, he added, that, according to Lily and Jack, at the time they'd wanted to wed, New York didn't permit first cousins to marry, so they'd eloped to New Jersey, which did.

I called Jessica and said something snippy about my hapless in-laws, and later I felt sorry and emailed her:

Jef's information was fascinating. I never knew any of this. Though can't help feeling Jack and Lily shouldn't have tried to get around the law by going to New Jersey. Still, it's all so long ago. I guess we just have to grin and bear it. Grin indeed—if you're related to the Marx Brothers. Maybe you are. Maybe that's where you (and your Pa) inherited your wit. Which would be the bright side of the cloud.

A few hours later I received this email from Jessica:

Dear Mom:
While I know egocentrism is one of the behavior problems that's common after a stroke, I can't help thinking that I, myself, am the bright side of the cloud. Given that my very existence would not have been possible without Jack and Lily and the state of New Jersey, I am not one to judge what they did. I will take blood clots and strokes over non-existence any day. Sure, you could have had a daughter in perfect health, with

*no possible genetic problems, but would you have wanted her
instead of me?*

Of course, she was right. I didn't want any daughter other than the
one I had. I just wanted, however unreasonably, to have her un-
damaged, and I'd yet to come to terms with what had happened. I
still wanted her perfect. No hesitancy in her walk. No braces.

I knew this from my dreams. I still dreamed regularly that Jessica was walking normally. In one recurring dream, I was huffing and
puffing to keep up with her the way I'd had to do when she, a teenager
bursting with youthful energy, was in a hurry to get somewhere and I,
already feeling my years, was struggling to match her swift gait.

I never told Jessica about these dreams, even though she'd told
me about her own dreams of walking on that now long ago August
day in Reeves. But one night, four years after her stroke, I had a
dream so vivid that while I was on the phone with her an account
of it just popped out of my mouth. I'd dreamt she and I were in our
kitchen on West End Avenue—the kitchen where I'd taught her to
cook, where we'd baked endless batches of cookies just the way she
now did with her own daughters. In the dream, Jessica was putting
dishes away and gossiping with me as she worked.

When I awoke, I was awash with sadness. "It seemed so real,"
was what hurtled from my lips. "The way you were walking around."

"I *am* walking around," Jessica said.

"I mean," I said, "in the dream you were doing it without braces."

"Big deal," Jessica responded. "So I walk with braces."

So I walk with braces. Her response made me remember a
passage that had struck me in a book I'd read earlier—the autobiography of Dr. Howard Rusk, the physician who is considered
the father of modern rehabilitation medicine. "You don't get fine
china by putting clay in the sun," Rusk wrote. "You have to put the
clay through the white heat of the kiln if you want to make porce-
lain. Heat breaks some pieces. Life breaks some people. Disability
breaks some people. But once the clay goes through the white-hot

fire and comes out whole, it can never be clay again; once a person overcomes a disability through his own courage, determination and hard work, he has a depth of spirit you and I know little about."

What I heard in Jessica's response the day I told her my kitchen dream was exactly what Rusk had described so eloquently: an astonishing depth of spirit. But it was to be a long while before I caught up with her ability to stop dreaming about what might have been and accept what was. It happened finally at a wedding not so very long ago. I've always been a sucker for weddings. I'm the ideal wedding guest: the relative or friend who can be counted on to cry when a couple takes their vows. So perhaps it was inevitable that it would be at a wedding, soon after shedding my tears of joy at beholding a new family forming, that I would finally have the transformative experience that would let me see *my* family—my daughter—in a different light, that would finally allow me to let my child lead me, instead of always expecting it to be the other way 'round.

The wedding was the marriage of Jessica's cousin Gregory, the cousin who'd been her age-mate, the one whose hand she'd grasped as, together, they'd taken their first steps. Greg lived in Japan, where he had met Keiko, the bride, but the wedding was held in Berkeley, California, where his mother lived. Jessica flew north from Texas, I flew west from New York, and we each took a room in the Women's Faculty Club, where, before the actual event, we sat around putting finishing touches on our outfits and chattering at length about the relatives we'd soon be seeing.

In addition to those relatives, Greg and Keiko had invited to their wedding friends from both Japan and the United States, and while not all of their friends spoke the same language, one language they all had in common was the music of the Beatles. After the afternoon campus ceremony and toward the end of the indoor dinner in a university club, the first Beatles tune began booming from speakers near an improvised dance floor, and, wherever they hailed from, all of the bride and groom's peers rose from their seats and began rocking and swirling on the smooth wooden floor. Out of consideration for Jessica, who as far as I knew didn't—couldn't—dance, I remained seated alongside her at our table. We chattered again about whatever came to mind—this aunt's appearance, that cousin's young sons. But, after a while, I had to excuse myself to go to the ladies' room.

When I returned, I didn't see Jessica at the table.

Where was she? My eyes swept the hall, and then turned to the swirling mass on the dance floor. There was Jessica, with her cane, rocking along with everyone else.

What a girl, I thought. It was a transcendent moment. One in which I finally was able to put aside fantasy and cherish—even more than the memory of the child my daughter had once been—the powerful person she had become.

What a girl, I thought. And then, proudly: And I'm her mother. ✒

Acknowledgments

FIRST AND FOREMOST, I'd like to thank my daughter, Jessica Wolfe Bernstein, who not only granted me permission to write about her and the events described in this book but provided staunch support during that writing and invaluable editing of the final draft. I'd like to thank Jon Bernstein as well, who was, and is, wiser by far than I. Thanks, too, to my granddaughters, Miriam and Rachel, whom I had to ask on occasion to fill me in on half-remembered details of some of their childhood activities.

I'm also grateful to my friends Ann Hurwitz and Elizabeth Shepherd for reading my earliest drafts, my friend Ted Friedman for legal hand-holding, my step-grandson Daniel Pollack-Pelzner for our many talks about literary matters, my stepdaughter Debby Pollack for her assistance throughout this family crisis, and my stepdaughter Jude Pollack for cheering me on once I began writing.

Speaking of writing, I would never have written this book without the help of my late husband, Max Pollack. He knew how much I wanted to tell the story of Jessica's stroke and its impact not just on me but on our whole family. He also knew I was afraid to write it because I had only rarely written in a personal vein. Being the phenomenal psychologist he was, Max said, "If you don't write this, you'll probably never write anything again." He challenged me, which got me started, championed me as I progressed, and read the first half of the manuscript shortly before he died, telling me to keep it up, it was going just fine.

Alas, I couldn't keep going after he died. For 35 years he'd been my mentor, my Main Man, my colleague in all my endeavors. For several years after his death, I kept trying to get back into this book, but it was to no avail. I tried, too, to write some articles, also to no avail. I was having my first-ever brush with writer's block.

Around that time, someone told me about a writing teacher whose students were all in the midst of writing nonfiction books. I'd never taken a writing course in my life, but I was at my wit's end. So, thinking I'd just sit around and audit, I signed up for a class with one Charles Salzberg, and, to my astonishment, Salzberg, a sorcerer, motivated me to take on—and ultimately enjoy—the difficult work of finishing the book. Recognizing that as a lifelong journalist I was used to deadlines, he provided them, and when I met them, he offered perceptive critiques of my mounting pages. My fellow students also offered encouragement, and many of them bedazzled me with sparkling editorial comments.

I also want to thank my dedicated, undauntable agent, Irene Skolnick, who never gave up on the book; my perspicacious editor, Gini Kopecky Wallace, who can lasso an unruly sentence and swiftly gentle it into cooperating; and Bob Lascaro, Greenpoint's uncommonly talented design director, who combed through forty years of family photos to find the one that inspired him to make the book's cover. Thanks, too, to John King, MD, Medical Director of Reeves Rehabilitation Center in San Antonio's University Hospital, who talked at length with me about the clinic and granted me permission to interview staff members, several of whom are featured in this book; Charles Stacy, MD, and Jesse Weinberger, MD, of Mount Sinai Hospital in New York City, who helped me decipher some of the neurology of stroke; and Lori Monson, PT, MSPC, OCS, of Bradley & Monson Physiotherapy in New York City for our many discussions about rehabilitation and for reading a late draft of the manuscript.

Finally, I am more grateful than I can ever say to Ellie Forland and Marvin Forland, MD, who lived through many of the events in this book with me. They were, and are, extraordinary foul-weather friends, and unbeatable fair-weather friends as well. ✍

Mother and daughter in New York City three and a half years
after Jessica's stroke, November 2005. *Photo by Max Pollack.*

About the Author

LINDA WOLFE IS AN AWARD-WINNING journalist and
novelist. Among her many books are the novel *Private Practices*, which she based on her investigations into the mysteri-
ous deaths of renowned twin gynecologists in New York City, and
numerous works about true crimes, including *Wasted: The Preppie
Murder*; *Love Me to Death*, a memoir about the murder of one of
Wolfe's friends; *The Professor and the Prostitute*, a collection of her
most notable crime pieces; and *The Murder of Dr. Chapman*, the
story of an early 19th-century school mistress accused of conspiring
with a lover to kill her scientist husband. Wolfe is also the author of
a classic work on food in literature, *The Literary Gourmet*.

A longtime contributing editor at *New York* magazine, Wolfe's
articles and personal essays have also appeared in *The New York
Times*, *Vanity Fair*, *Playboy*, and many other major publications.

Her short fiction has appeared in *Southwest Review, The University of Kansas City Review,* and other literary journals. She has been a frequent judge for the National Book Critics Circle annual awards, and is currently the book critic for the website FabOverFifty.

Learn more at LindaWolfe.com.